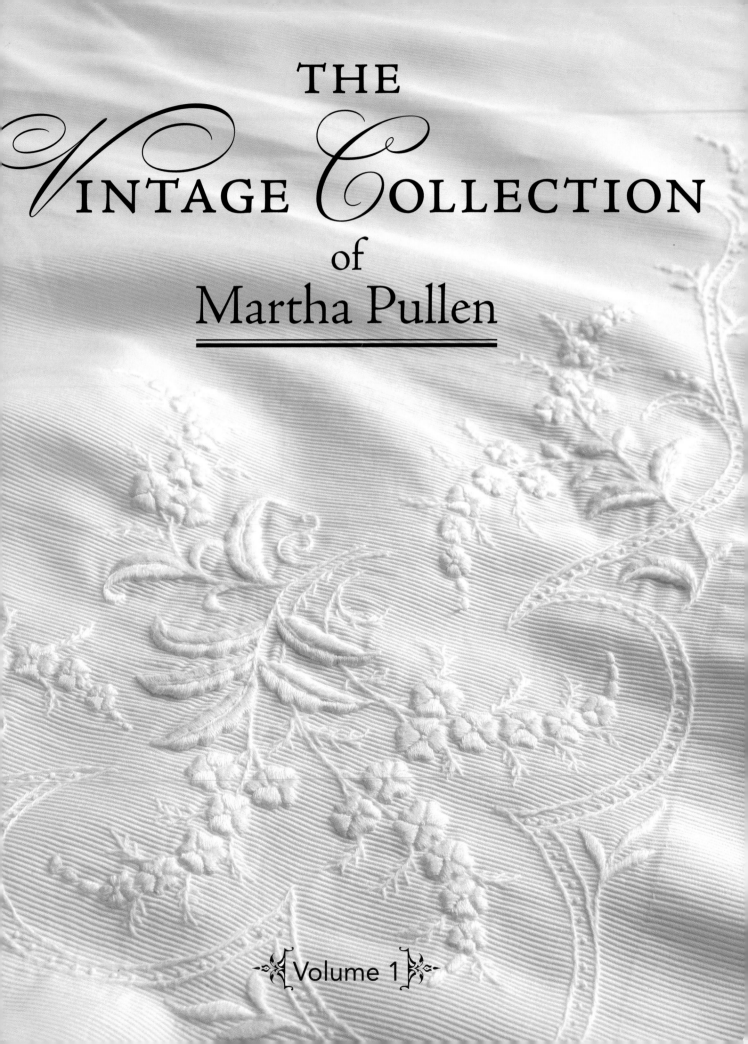

THE
VINTAGE COLLECTION
of
Martha Pullen

Volume 1

Dedication

The Martha Pullen collection of vintage embroideries and garments is a sewing journey. Martha began collecting these garments to use as examples for designs, sewing technique, and inspiration for her own designs. Traveling throughout the world leads Martha on her never-ending search for examples of fine sewing. With each addition to the collection, a piece of history has been preserved for us today. The collection contains garments from many countries with the belief that the garments should be preserved for today and tomorrow.

The delicate pieces of fabric, lace and ribbons are orchestrated to meet style demands and utilitarian purposes for the wearer of the day. Discarded by generations, these garments in the hand of a dedicated collector became prized possessions. Martha, by painstakingly caring for these garments, honors women from past generations who made them.

The Martha Pullen Collection, Martha's delightful stories about her search, and the history of these garments has intrigued me for years. Just as finding a breathtaking garment stirs the soul, so does the passionate storytelling of the collector, as she tells the story of each piece. Martha is passionate about her antique garments. They come to life when she dreams of the wearer and puts herself into the maker's shoes. The insight to preserve these fabulous finds is admirable. But more importantly, sharing them with each of us through these pages is invaluable.

I have chosen to dedicate this book to Martha Pullen, even though it is written by her, for her years of inspiring us to make beautiful garments. As the fabrics, sewing machines, ribbons, buttons, and embellishments have changed through the years, the love of sewing has remained the same. She has inspired many of us to love our handwork, seam by seam, ribbon by ribbon and stitch by stitch.

I have known Martha Pullen since she started her business. Her love of beautiful things stems from her beautiful heart. As she shares her collection with you, she is sharing her heart…full of love for God, her family, and her friends, for which I am thankful to be one.

Phyllis Laxton Hoffman

Phyllis Hoffman
Publisher

Table of Contents

For Joe Pullen

My partner, my husband, my traveling companion, and best friend.

—Martha

The Martha Pullen Company

Author:
Martha Pullen
The Martha Pullen Company
149 Old Big Cove Road
Brownsboro, Alabama 35741
www.marthapullen.com

Editorial Direction by Kathy McMakin
Editorial Contribution by Amelia Johanson
Embroidery Design by Angela Pullen Atherton

Hoffman Media, LLC.

Publisher:
Phyllis Hoffman
Hoffman Media, LLC.
1900 International Park Drive, Suite 50
Birmingham, Alabama 35243

Production Direction by Greg Baugh
Graphic Design by Jordan Marxer
Photography by Daren Whitaker
Color Correction by Delisa McDaniel
Photostyling by Lindsay Keith
Copy Editing by Wanda Billings

Printed in the United States of America
ISBN: 0-9770069-090000

Preface

It was my mother who taught me to appreciate fine sewing, beautiful seams, bound buttonholes, inside finishes and intricate embroidery – garments that were beautifully constructed inside and out. When I think back, however, I believe my fascination with historical clothing began while I was in college. I majored in speech and literature and acted in a number of plays, and what I remember most about the performances were the period costumes. I learned then that "costume" is the correct word for period clothing, although I still find it hard to say that I love Victorian "costume" rather than Victorian "clothing."

Fast forward years later to when I turned my love of sewing into an heirloom business. Everything we did to develop heirloom sewing by machine was rooted in the fine craftsmanship of the white antique clothing that was generations old. I began to pick up a dress here, a bonnet there, and many slips along the way. By studying these pieces of history, I could bring the delicate art of yesterday's sewing to today's world of technologically advanced machines. I dipped into the past not only to borrow technique, but design. Antiques from my collection have inspired my middy dress patterns, my basic yoke dress, and all of my women's blouses and nightgowns.

During my first trip to England, I must have purchased 30 baby dresses at the antique shops along Portabella Road. I wanted to enjoy every seam inside those dresses, every sewing detail, and the more I looked over them, the more I realized white clothing, or should I say "costume" was going to be my passion. I toured the Victoria and Albert Museum and committed to memory every white baby gown I could take in. I simply drank in the stark beauty of everything there, and I saw for the first time authentic women's clothing from the Victorian and Edwardian era. I had seen similar pieces along Portabella Road, but was so taken with the baby clothing that I hadn't really paid much attention to the adult things. What I mistakenly had assumed were old wedding dresses were actually white lingerie dresses, which were once worn as everyday clothing. Women wore white blouses with dark skirts as well as stark white dresses embellished with lace shaping and embroidery. It didn't take long before I was back on Portobello Road gathering up as many beautiful adult examples as I could find.

Daisy & Crossed Pintucked Blouse
American, circa 1910

I almost called this blouse my UFO (unfinished object) blouse because I truly believe it was never finished. I cannot, even underneath my magnifying glass, find any indication that closings were ever part of the construction process. Although we use beauty pins to close the backs of baby dresses and even children's dresses, I have never heard of their use on adult apparel. There are no buttonholes, nor is there any evidence that hooks and eyes were applied. The design incorporates a hidden placket down the back, but there never appears to have been any functional closure underneath.

The front and back of blouse are tucked in a checkerboard fashion with 1/8 inch wide overlapping pintucks, spaced 1 inch apart. Each square created by the tucked pattern holds a satin stitch embroidery, either a daisy or a dot. The eye catches the work in two ways – vertically, the daisies and dots appear in alternating rows; horizontally, the daisies and dots alternate every other square.

The blouse was machine made, although the embroidery was most definitely worked by hand. The stand-up collar measures 1-1/2 inches deep. It is a single row of the pintucked fabric squares, which alternate with the daisies and dots. French edging trims the very top of the collar and travels down the back placket opening, just to where the collar joins the blouse. The cuffs of the sleeves were cut from the same pintucked and embroidered fabric. Including the 5/8 inch wide gathered lace edging, they are approximately 5 inches deep, which incorporates three rows of alternating squares and a half row that is unadorned. The edging travels around the hem of the cuff then sharply turns upward to run the entire length giving the impression that hidden buttons are beneath. There are no buttons or a closure of any kind; the lace is purely decorative.

The fullness of the blouse is gathered in with a flat cording, which ties off to the side in back.

The beauty of this, and most blouses of this era, is that the embellishment is carried around from front to back. Attention to detail was critical in the making of a woman's blouse, so that the wearer was a vision coming and going.

Double V Mystery Baby Dress
Scottish, circa 1880

The Double V Mystery Baby Dress caught my eye in a little shop full of odds and ends in Edinburgh, Scotland. Amidst what is best described as junk were several pieces of very pretty white Victorian clothing, one of which was a batiste dress trimmed with Swiss embroidery and French laces.

This is one of my more interesting pieces because I am absolutely positive that the same person did not make the skirt and bodice. The most apparent difference is the trim work on the bodice and the skirt. The top was made from Swiss trims using machine stitching. The lace insertions on the handmade skirt are French, with the possible exception of the bottom piece of lace, which could be English.

The basic round neckline was fashioned with a casing and gathering cord to adjust the size appropriately to the child who was wearing it. Just below the neckline, Swiss insertion was positioned vertically down the yoke and flanked by two side panels of edging. Two mitered Vs of insertion were placed directly on top of the previous work and outlined with a Swiss binding trim and a slightly gathered Swiss edging. Six pieces of Swiss binding trim—the longest applied just inside the mitered edging and the tiniest next to the neckline casing—were shaped in graduating V to fill in the neckline

area above each mitered insertion V. The same Swiss binding trim was applied to either side of the Swiss insertion waistband.

The back of the bodice was left unadorned except for the Swiss edging gathered all around the neckline to the opening. The puffed sleeves were trimmed with the Swiss binding and the same slightly gathered French lace edging that was used around the neckline. The placket opening in the back of the dress is 11 inches long. The only closure in the back is the draw cords at the neckline and at the waistline.

The skirt was made in a different manner. It was constructed completely by hand from the inside seams to the tiny stitches attaching the lace. The tucks are 3/8 inches wide and were spaced 3/8 inches apart. There are three sets of three tucks, and the measurement from where the tucks begin to the bottom of the skirt is 12 inches. Two pieces of round thread French lace insertion were applied in-between the three sets of tucks. Even the hem, which is 1-5/8 inches wide, was secured with the tiniest of hand stitches. Because of the significant differences in both materials and type of construction used to make the bodice and skirt, I am positive that two different people, possibly from two different eras, worked on the dress.

Pink Silk Dressing Sack

French, circa 1915-1930

In *The Delineator*, April, 1904 short blouse-like garments fell under the category of "dressing sacks." One such garment was described in the following manner. *"Shrimp pink flannel and white lawn were employed for the construction of the simple dressing-sack here displayed, fancy stitching forming the trimming in one instance and the ribbon and lace edging in the other."*

This charming piece might have been a dressing sack or it could be from a later era, when it would have been called a bed jacket. When I was a child, every women had what we called bed jackets. Mama always put one on when she went to bed at night while she read. My grandmother had several bed jackets, all brand new mind you, in her "hospital drawer." Actually my grandmother never went to the hospital, but nearly all of the women in my family had a "hospital drawer" filled with nice gowns and bed jackets. In their eras, when you went to the hospital, you generally stayed there for some time. My mother was in the hospital for 10 days after my birth; and even I stayed in the hospital for seven days with my first child.

Whether this pink silk jacket was originally called a dressing sack, a combing coat, or a bed jacket, I'm honestly not sure, because I haven't been able to determine when it was constructed.

The pink silk is relatively sturdy and has a lovely hand. That jacket is made up of two front panels and a back panel; the only connecting seam is on the shoulders, and it is a French seam. A row of 1/2 inch wide French insertion and slightly gathered 1 inch wide ecru French edging trims the entire jacket. The laces are ecru. The trim goes all the way around the neckline, down both sides, around the bottom of the front pieces, up the side panels, down the back side panels and around the back of the jacket. The side panels close under the arm with a tiny button stitched through both pieces of the lace, which fashions an "armhole." When I first examined this feature on the jacket it appeared as if there were a buttonhole applied so that the side could be left completely open; there wasn't. The button was simply stitched on to permanently hold both layers together.

Five 6-1/4 inch long released pintucks gather in a bit of the fullness at the shoulder. The shoulder seam measures 6 inches from the neck to the edge of the "sleeve." The measurement from where the ribbon ties to the edge of the sleeve is 8-1/4 inches. You can see that the pintucks took up 2 inches of space on the panel and helped to shape the jacket. The bottom was cut in a slight flair and measures 9 inches across. The total length of the jacket is 20 inches.

The pink ribbons were first tied in a bow then stitched down to the edge of the opening leaving the ribbon tails to tie the jacket closed. This jacket would be very easy to make. If you cut loose the button and untied it, the entire piece would lay out completely flat. It is was made on a straight stitch sewing machine and the laces were simply overlapped slightly and stitched together with a straight stitch.

$\mathcal{L}$ace Poetry Blouse
English, circa 1900

The most ingenious and ephemeral of textiles ever created, lace is truly the poetry of fashion…There is no definitive answer as to how and why lace developed or what source provided the inspiration for its creation. Perhaps it was the shadows of the trees in summer, or snow-covered twigs in winter, or the swimming, rhythmic movements of the clouds, or a spider's web, or even the seaweed and shells caught in a fisherman's net.

—Bella Neksler, *Lace, the Poetry of Fashion*

I find this blouse pure poetry. It's from a London shop in Camden Passage, an area past Angel Tube Station that is preserved entirely for trade in antiques, crafts and clothes. The windows are appealing, and many times I have found beautiful white Victorian clothing staring out at me from behind the panes. This was the case with my Lace Poetry Blouse.

Part of the blouse is made from very thin white Swiss batiste and part is made from dotted Swiss. The blouse features 1/16 inch wide tucks placed horizontally across the yoke and broken up by vertically placed lengths of 5/8 inch wide French lace insertion. The work on the yoke somewhat resembles a spider's web radiating from the wide neckband. The neckband consists of a strip of the 5/8 inch wide insertion, a section of batiste that was positioned so that the tucks lie at an angle, a second piece of 5/8 inch wide insertion, a bias binding and a gathered piece of lace edging at the very top. In all, the neckband stands 3 inches tall.

Outlining the yoke are sections of beautiful Swiss embroidery. Floral strips were hand hemstitched across the bottom of the yoke, and over each shoulder. A single flower and leaf motif was applied at center front. Gathered lace edging was then added around the outside edge of the entire Swiss addition.

The center panel of the blouse is dotted Swiss fashioned across with release tucks. The section beneath the dotted Swiss is best described as two rows of geometric lace shaping above and below a section of tucked batiste, which like the collar was positioned so that the tucks are running at an angle.

The lowermost portion of the blouse is an unadorned section of dotted Swiss gathered to a dotted Swiss waistband.

The full sleeves are equally ornate and echo the lacework on the blouse. The sleeve is dotted Swiss drawn in by a series of tucks to the cuff. A run of geometric lace shaping was applied directly on top of the tucked area, framing an insert of angled tucks. The actual cuff was made identically to the collar.

The back details are very similar to the front affirming this blouse a masterpiece. It closes with 15 buttons and loops. The blouse was constructed by machine. The inside seams are French.

In fashion, lace is, above all, a symbol of *poetry and femininity.*

—Bella Neksler, *Lace, The Poetry of Fashion*

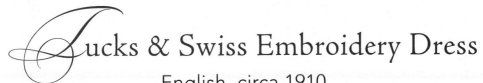

Tucks & Swiss Embroidery Dress
English, circa 1910

Christie's on Old Brompton Road in London holds only one or two textile auctions a year. It's almost as if I've missed a holiday if I can't get to them. Fortunately, when they auctioned off the Tucks and Swiss Embroidery Dress, I was present. This exquisitely hand stitched, white batiste dress was one in an assortment of baby clothes referred to as a "lot." Usually in these "lots" there are one or two fabulous pieces, some ordinary things and several that could almost be discarded. This piece alone was worth the price of the entire lot, regardless of what else was in it. It is a masterpiece for those who love sewing.

This piece alone was worth the price of the entire lot, regardless of what else was in it. It is a masterpiece for those who love sewing.

Let me start with the bodice, which was fashioned with exquisite Swiss trims and tucks, but not just any tucks. The tucks on this piece were brilliantly placed at a slight diagonal and hand stitched with precision. A length of Swiss beading, 3/4 inch wide, was applied around the bottom of the bodice through which ribbon was run and tied into a sash in the back. A narrow, bias strip was applied around the neckline, further trimmed with a 1/2 inch wide gathered French edging and topped with tiny French knots.

The back of the dress was made exactly like the front except for the placket, which is completely hidden and further conceals four buttons and buttonholes underneath. Only when the dress is unbuttoned is there any noticeable difference between the front and back.

The join of the shoulder seams preserves the tiniest piping, covered, of course, with the Swiss batiste fabric from the dress. The long sleeves were set in with this same tiny piping using a rolled and whipped technique. A fancy band, also hand applied, served to finish the sleeve with a combination of Swiss trim, a row of Swiss insertion and a row of slightly gathered French lace edging, which matches that used around the neckline. In order to make this sleeve fit a little more snug around the child's arm, a tiny pearl button and a little handmade button loop were placed 1-1/2 inches apart on the middle of the cuff. There is no placket just this button and button loop. It is the one and only time I've seen this treatment on a baby dress.

The skirt was fashioned with three rows of three tucks, a beautiful Swiss insertion with entredeux on both sides, and a ruffle made from a slightly gathered, 3 inch wide Swiss edging. The handstitched tucks were folded to a width of 1/8 inch and were spaced 1/8 inch apart; the sets of tucks were spaced 3/8 inch apart.

The back dress length is 21-1/2 inches, and the circumference of the skirt is 71 inches.

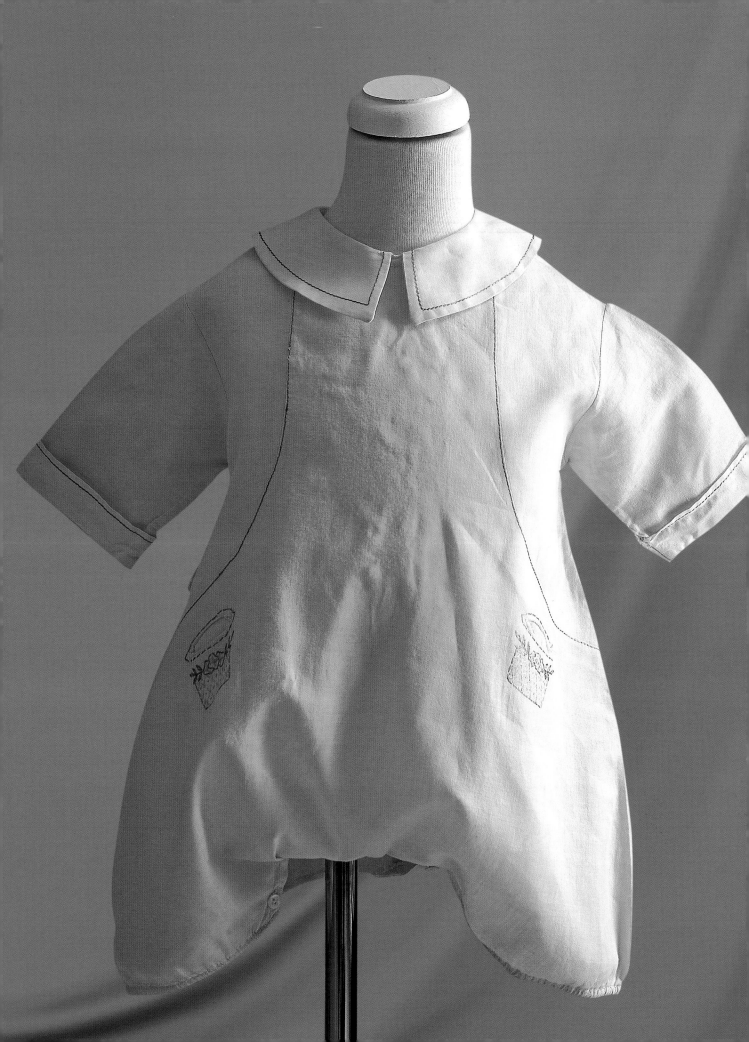

Boy's Yellow Romper
American, circa 1920

A little yellow linen romper for baby boy is the epitome of cool charm during those ever-so-hot summer months. I purchased this piece in Lebanon, Ohio. It, indeed, has the "touch of handwork" that *Modern Priscilla* (1918) so cleverly encouraged in the passage below. A touch of handwork is still pleasant to see on children's clothing and the effect it provides can now be achieved quickly and easily on a sewing machine with embroidery capabilities.

The suit style is basically a center panel, flanked by two side panels. Two tiny oval pocket openings on either side of the front panel are outlined in brown topstitching. A geometric and flower design in yellow, ecru and brown was handworked directly on top of the pocket space. This is the most unusual little child's pocket I have ever seen.

Brown topstitching follows the line of the join between the center and side panels. It also outlines the shape of the Bermuda collar. The collar and cuffs are ecru linen. The set-in sleeves are finished with a narrow cuff and topstitched in brown thread 1/4 inch from the upper edge.

There are two belt loops on the side of the suit and my guess would be that a belt, which double buttoned was run through these loops and worn across the back only to hold in some of the suit's fullness. The front is embellished such that a belt would have distracted from the decorative pockets and topstitching.

The suit buttons at the crotch with four buttons and buttonholes. The buttonholes are on the front; the buttons are on the back. Elastic was used around the legs to gather in the fullness. The back of the suit has two plain panels and a placket, which measures 6 inches long; this is plenty long enough to easily slide over a wiggly boy's head. The back placket closes with two buttonholes and buttons.

*E*very mother wants her children to be well dressed and she knows that the hall-mark of attractive clothes…is handwork. And yet, 'How can I spend the time embroidering when there is such a need in the world?' is the very next thought. But that difficulty is quickly settled by choosing either garments that are made up all ready to put on when the handwork has been done, or by taking the utmost advantage of the simplicity that now marks fashionable attire for big and little people. Few seams, straight lines, frank and simple closings all conspire to take the dread out of dressmaking.

— *Modern Priscilla*, March, 1918

Bows & Flowers Woman's Camisole
America, circa 1900

It never ceases to amaze me that undergarments such as this camisole with intricate detail and handwork were viewed as everyday apparel in the early 1900s. A reproduction blouse, nightgown, camisole or even a baby dress would be beautiful using this delicate embroidery, but it would mostly certainly not be considered an everyday piece. Women always wore a slip or a camisole underneath their clothing until recent times. When corsets were worn, women also wore something underneath the corset. Can you imagine layering three undergarments before you even donned your dress?

The padded satin stitch flowers and bow design on this particular piece were worked on both fronts of the camisole and again at the center back. Hand scallops formed with a buttonhole stitch were meticulously worked all the way around the neckline, down both sides of the front, and around the armscyes. A strip of a beautiful Swiss beading, through which ribbon is run to cinch in the camisole, defines the waistline. Eyelets worked in sets of two completely around the neckline serve the same purpose; ribbon is woven through them to pull up the fullness and to tie the camisole closed at the top. The bottom was finished with a 1/4 inch wide hem secured with a running stitch. The seams are French, and the whole camisole was made entirely by hand.

Victorian camisoles have long been a passion of mine for two reasons. The first is the creative way they utilized lace and Swiss embroidered embellishment, and the second is for the gorgeous embroidery. When lingerie dresses came into fashion, of course, decorative camisoles and slips were a necessity. What were lingerie dresses? They were somewhat sheer white day dresses. The materials used to make them —batiste, lace and Swiss embroideries—had been reserved before 1880 for sewing lingerie; therefore, lingerie dresses were quite the modern trend and a little bit daring for the time.

Front Opening Piqué Christening Dress

English, circa 1910

I purchased the Front Opening Piqué Christening Dress at an antique store on King's Road, and honestly my first thought was, "Exactly what is this?" The shop owner explained that it was a style of christening dress that would have been worn with a beautiful under dress or possibly an ornate slip. Made of sturdy piqué, and lined with Swiss broadcloth, it is heavier than most of my christening gowns. Equally heavy, but truly magnificent is the padded satin stitch embroidery, which was worked from the yoke of the dress, down to the bottom and all the way around the skirt. The white-on-white embroidery is an array of densely stitched leaves, stems and beautiful sprays of flowers intertwined with winding scrolls that were worked in double rows of outline stitches with French knots in-between. The scrolls somewhat resemble ribbons. Similar embroidery was worked completely around the 2 inch wide cuffs.

Three wide pleats contain the fullness in the front. A 3 inch wide Swiss edging tops the two innermost pleats on either side of the front opening. The Swiss trim was stitched flat down the front then gathered around the bottom and all the way around the back. The neckline and the bottom of the yokes, front and back were finished with very tiny piping .

The back of the dress also has three wide pleats on each side of the placket, to hold in the fullness. The back yoke opening plus the placket is 9 inches long. The dress closes with two buttons and button loops. The length of this dress is 36 inches. The circumference of the skirt is 66 inches including the width of the Swiss trims.

I do wish I had the dress or slip, which went underneath this christening dress. I wonder if it were as ornately embroidered. Here is a tip from one heirloom lover to, I assume, another: If the slip and gown are not tacked together before storing, there is a great probability the slip will be misplaced. Start a tradition of tacking the slip to the christening gown at the shoulders before washing and storing. This way both pieces will survive together for generations to come.

Custom has long decreed white for the first dresses, and even in the present riot of color, it is still the unquestioned selection for the newcomer.

— *Modern Priscilla*, July, 1922

Embroidered Netting Christening Cape
French, circa 1900

Every time I look at one of my French garments, I am reminded why France, or more specifically Paris, is the cradle of fashion. The French have always expressed themselves through art and style. Even garments for the very small are in a class of their own. This rare find from the Paris Flea Market is a brilliant christening coat with an attached cape.

The eye first settles on the floral embroidery above the deep hem of the cape, and is immediately drawn up to the three rows of narrow puffing encircling the neck and shoulders. A French edging ruffle carries the eye gently down the front opening of both the cape and coat exposing more floral work on the under layer. The three rows of puffing are 5/8 inch wide and are separated by a 1/8 inch wide French insertion lace. The cape is gathered to the bottom of the puffing and insertion treatment. It is trimmed down the front with French insertion and gathered edging. The cape hem and the lining hem are 3-1/4 inches wide; the hem at the bottom of the coat is 3-1/2 inches.

The basic coat underneath the cape is netting, which was attached at all of the seams with a pretty, delicate French lace trim, which resembles faggoting. The trim repeats on the bottom of the long sleeves where it is combined with a tiny row of puffing 1/4 inch wide and French edging. The actual skirt of the coat is a delicately embroidered netting piece, which would have been sold as wide goods by the yard. I can't determine whether the embroidered netting was French, English or Swiss made. All of these countries made gorgeous netting laces by the yard. The cape was also cut from the embroidered netting.

One of the most unusual features of this coat is that it is lined in plain netting. The lining is tacked in several places along the front. The coat closes with three pearl buttons and three button loops. The complete garment was constructed by hand. The coat length is 23 inches. The cape length is 15 inches. The sleeve length is 8 inches. While a straight line of hand embroidery was used to hem the bottom of the coat and the cape, the companion embroidery on the coat was applied on the netting at the factory.

Drawstring Petticoat with Crochet & Cluny Lace
French, circa 1900

"Bonjour, Madame," said the slender Frenchman in the booth in the Paris Flea Market. I answered, "Bonjour, " pointed to several white pieces in this man's booth and asked "Combien (how much)?" He apparently determined that I'd exhausted my knowledge of the French language, and to my relief replied with written prices in francs. After I'd purchased what I liked, he led me to another vendor who dealt in similar antique clothing. Through a passerby who was kind enough to act as an interpreter, I learned that this second vendor had more items at home, and he inquired as to whether I'd like him to bring them to my hotel. The following day, the vendor arrived at our elegant suite overlooking the Louvre, dragging with him several black garbage bags filled with white clothing. He pulled out item after item, dirty and dirtier, and placed them on the bed, the floor, the sofa and the chairs. I selected a number of pieces—knowing from experience that the more I purchased, the better the prices would be—one of which was this beautiful petticoat typical of the Victorian period.

Since part of my love for these garments is imagining their origin, I'd like to think that the seamstress made her petticoat using some handmade crochet lace made by someone in her family and filled in with a wider Cluny insertion and edging she had in her stash. The laces indeed look beautiful together, and I would encourage you to blend different types of laces in your sewing. It adds interest to your work as it did on this heavy broadcloth petticoat made more than 100 years ago.

Hemstitch machines were invented in the mid 1800s, and this petticoat features three 1/2 inch wide tucks on the first tier, which were stitched down with machine hemstitching. The first piece of hand crocheted lace was straight stitched underneath the bottom tuck, leaving barely any space between the tucks. The second piece of crocheted lace was attached to the bottom of a tuck in the second tier of the petticoat, which also has a 4 inch wide ruffle. On the lowest tier, a ruffle was applied under which lies a 2-1/4 inch wide piece of French Cluny insertion underneath, followed by a 2 inch wide band of fabric, and a 3-1/2 inch wide piece of Cluny edging to finish the bottom. The circumference around the largest part of the bottom of this petticoat is 120 inches; the length is 34 inches. The top closes with a 3/4 inch wide casing and a drawstring. All the seams in the petticoat are flat felled.

> I would like to think that this seamstress made her petticoat using some handmade crochet lace made by someone in her family and filled in with a wider Cluny insertion and edging she had in her stash.

English Middy Overlay Dress

English, circa 1900

True London antique buffs refer to shopping Portobello Road as "Saturday on the Portobello." Every Saturday morning in every kind of weather, the long, winding Portobello Road on Notting Hill attracts thousands of visitors. I have heard so many languages spoken there. I have seen "street people," and I have seen the moneyed dressed in the finest Italian furs sporting diamonds as large as headlights. It is an experience in diversity. Around 7 am or shortly thereafter, merchants begin to assemble their street stalls. The real "find" has nowadays become an increasing rarity, partly because press and television coverage of antiques and collecting has led many people to appreciate and in some cases overvalue their possessions. One can define "find" in many ways. This dress was, quite frankly, expensive, but I think worth it. It is not only beautiful to behold, it was beautifully constructed.

The Swiss embroidery that is sewn in columns down the overlay is indescribably lovely. The top part of the design is graduated white-on-white circles followed by three flowers, one slightly larger than the next. The center section begins with two basic leaves, under which is an undefined shape that looks almost like an ivy leaf embellished with vertical lines of satin stitching. Beneath that is a satin stitched bow and a tiny half wreath of flowers. The bottom design is a large white rose mingling with tiny daisies beneath an oval design again filled with vertical lines of satin stitching.

There are six sets of this same Swiss embroidered design on the three-paneled overlay; two on each panel with five released tucks in between. The tucks are very narrow, almost pintucks spaced 1/8 inch apart. The original embroidery was likely purchased in a wide piece and later cut by the seamstress to suit her overlay design.

French insertion outlines each of the three overlay panels and serves to join them together. Each panel is curved at the bottom so when joined a scallop line is created. A coordinating French edging was lightly gathered and applied around the scallops.

The overlay panels measure 3-1/2 inches wide at the bottom and 3 inches wide at the top. The length of the panels is 13-1/2 inches, which includes the lace finish.

The square neckline is trimmed with a narrow French lace insertion that was mitered at the corners and stitched on straight. This dress was constructed mostly by machine except where entredeux was used to attach the sleeves to the armscye. The sleeve fullness is controlled with three sets of three released pintucks 5 inches long placed 1/4 inch apart; there is a 5/8 inch wide space between the sets of pintucks. Envisioning the sleeve laid out flat, it was constructed of three pieces; a middle panel rounded at the bottom like those on the overlay sandwiched between two pieces of plain fabric. French insertion, applied around the center panel, joins all three pieces so that when the sleeve was set into the garment, the lace curves beautifully up into the armscye. French lace was softly gathered around the bottom.

The skirt overlay, like the bodice, is a series of panels curved along the bottom, joined together with 1 inch wide lace insertion, and finished with slightly gathered edging. The panels measure 8 by 5-1/2 inches wide. Swiss entredeux was inserted at the side seams of the overlay skirt panels. Since the seamstress wouldn't have had a zigzag sewing machine, the laces were placed underneath the lace or on top of the fabric and applied with a straight machine stitch.

The underskirt, which was gathered at the dropped waistline and sewn into the dress with the overlay skirt, was trimmed with 1 inch wide French insertion placed 4-1/4 inches from the bottom. The same insertion finishes the very bottom and was joined with an application of French lace edging that is so slightly gathered it appears flat. The total length of the underskirt is 15 inches.

The back of this dress has two rows of the white insertion with 10 released pintucks traveling over to meet the center back. The pintucks are 8 inches long. The shoulder seams are French as are the inside seams of the dress. The back closes with five buttons and buttonholes and a hook and eye at the top of the neckline. The total back length of the dress is 32 inches long. The circumference of the dress is 72 inches.

As a rule, lace is more satisfactorily applied to a garment if whipped on by and by. In some cases, however, this method is impractical, especially when a garment is trimmed with many ruffles. If lace is to be stitched to a garment by the sewing machine, be certain that a loose tension is employed; then, just before completing the work, tighten the tension. This will ensure an even edge and prevent the lace from ripping.

—To Sew Lace, Mrs. L.R.
Illustrated Needlework, May, 1923

Pintucks & Lace Combing Coat
English, circa 1900

Several antique stores in Bath, England specialize in white Victorian clothing. I cannot be sure of the location of the shop where I purchased this white batiste combing coat, but I believe it was somewhere on Union Street or Northumberland Place.

The sewing of lovely lingerie was written about in nearly all of the women's magazines during the early 1900s. The June issue of *The Delineator* in 1903 shared some interesting thoughts on the motivation behind sewing lingerie.

"The cost of lingerie is greater than a few years ago, but when one considers the exquisite fabrics and the quantity of lace and handwork, the expenditure is not out of proportion. Laces and ribbons are used in profusion, the former having preference over embroideries unless these are of the sheer, French variety. Daintiness should be the marked characteristic of lingerie, and where the expenditure of a limited amount of money is a consideration, it is wise to choose the finest of materials and decorate with handwork only. Ruffles with hemstitched hems and tucks, and the application of feather or brier stitching in scrolls or fanciful designs, are only a few suggestions of the ways in which lingerie may be decorated."

This combing coat uses lace and ruffles in profusion. The fabric is batiste and the laces are French. The rounded, almost petal collar features sets of five released 2-3/4-inch-long pintucks separated by sections of 1-inch beading. Beading is a lace insertion with "holes" intentionally woven down the center of the design through which ribbon is run. The French call beading "ribbon slot." The pintucks on the back of the collar extend to a measurement of 3 inches. Although some of the ribbons are missing from this beautiful collar it was apparent from the original ones still in the coat that they were attached at the collar

and secured in little folded bows where the gathered lace met the collar. The fabric portion of the collar is about 4 inches wide with the most gorgeous 3 inch wide French edging attached. The finished back edge of the collar is 7 inches.

Pintucks, spaced 5/8 inch apart, were run down the bulk of the sleeve and served to tame the fullness. French beading was applied below the pintucked fabric onto which was attached a full flounce. This flounce consists of a fabric section of released pintucks measuring 1-1/4 inches long and spaced 1/2 inch apart, followed by a 2-3/4 inch wide French edging. The beading, the tucked section and the edging were straight stitched onto the sleeve. The 2-3/4  inch French edging used on the sleeves was gathered to the bottom of the jacket as well as to the right of front portion of the coat.

A magnificent V-shaped panel of batiste, insertion and gathered 3-inch French edging was apparently made as a separate piece and then straight stitched to the entire jacket. The batiste Vs were outlined in French beading, which was straight stitched on and then mitered at each corner. The wide French edging was once again straight stitched following the V shape of the mitered beading. Fullness at the bottom V served to keep the shaped treatment from cupping under. French seams were used throughout the construction of this combing coat, which was made totally by machine.

Netting Dress with Grapes
French, circa 1920

I came across this white netting dress while searching through stalls at the Paris Flea Market. The leaves and grapes were formed from a double braid, which is about 1/16 inch wide. All the embroidery is done using this braid.

Six french knots make up each grape. While it appears that each grape has many strands per stitch, the double cord braid gives this illusion, it is actually one braid wrapped once. The leaves and stems are stitched using the same braid and couched throughout to hold the braid in place. The embroidery is done by hand.

The dress is 30 inches long and appears to be about a size 5. The grape embroidery was carried over to the kimono sleeves. The hem on the sleeves is 1-1/2 inch wide and was finished with strips of the double cord braid. The braid was not applied flat, but rather tied in three knots at 1-inch intervals. Individual knots in sets of three were spaced 1/8 inch apart. The neckline was finished with the same knotted braid trim, as was the placket in the back of the dress, which is 5 inches long. Two lengths of the knotted braid run completely around the skirt 2-1/4 inches below the grapes, and 3 inches above the hemline. The trim also holds in the waistline gathers, which extend from the straight 6 inch wide center panel all the way around to the back of the dress. In each case, the knotted braid was applied to the dress with hand stitching.

There are two beautiful leaf designs on the front bodice, and eight large sets of grapes and leaves on the skirt. The back of the dress is closed with a round button and a loop. The dress was completely constructed by hand.

When inspecting this dress, it is amazing that heavy braid was used on the delicate netting. Great care was taken to insure that the netting was not pulled while embroidering. Even when the braid was passed through the netting, there was no distortion of the fabric. This type of raised, knotted embroidery, could never have been reproduced on an embroidery machine, but the stunning hand embroidery designs can be reproduced.

Linen Dress with Embroidery & Cluny Lace
circa 1900

My grandmother used to talk about "substantial clothes, substantial people, and substantial furniture." My family has always valued quality clothing and fewer outfits rather than a closet full of poorly made things, and I still hold those values close to my heart. This dress is a perfect example of what my grandmother would have called substantial, and it was achieved through much effort. The details represent hours and hours of work. The linen is heavier than most of my garments, which are batiste. The lace is Cluny, which is rarely found in beautifully embroidered pieces of this generation, since usually the finer, more delicate French laces were used. Possibly, this dress was made for the winter season or for a colder climate. The linen and Cluny would have been more durable than the traditional fabrics.

The key design element is the lacework, and the mitered shapes, which were used throughout. The geometry of diamond shapes plays off beautifully against the V-shaped lace bodice that was intricately fashioned from Cluny lace, cutwork, tucks and white-on-white embroidery. Of the three large Vs on the yoke, the middle, mitered V is 12 inches down from the neckline. At the sides of the V treatment are three folded 1/4 inch wide tucks placed 1/4 inch apart; the tucks are 4-1/2 inches long. Six folded released tucks, 1/4 inch wide, 5/8 inch apart and 1 inch long, further ease in the yoke fullness.

A row of Cluny lace and four mitered Cluny lace V shapes add interest to the waistline. The smaller Vs enclose two 1/2 inch long darts. The tiny waistline measure only 23 inches.

The skirt incorporates a grid work of tucks running both vertically and horizontally fashioned around the front panel of three lace Vs and a lace diamond. The lace diamond is shaped around cutwork and white work embroidery. The sides of the skirt consist of 29 horizontal tucks, 1/8 inch wide and spaced 5/8 inch apart followed by 14 vertical released tucks, 1/4 inch wide and spaced 1/2 inch apart, flanked by a row of Cluny lace. The final touch is three identical shaped diamonds on each side of the front panel. The back skirt has a section of tucks and Cluny lace on each side.

The sleeves are made up of two mitered, Cluny lace Vs, cutwork and white work embroidery. The puffed sleeve is secured to the bodice with a 1/8 inch wide self-binding. The wide sleeve cuff, which has several rows of Cluny lace trim and three 1/4 inch wide tucks spaced 3/4 inch apart, is finished with a row of flat Cluny edging at the bottom.

The back bodice is made with four lace Vs featuring cutwork, white work embroidery and Cluny lace. It has six 1/4 inch wide tucks spaced 1/4 inch apart. The bodice is closed with a hook and eye at the neckline, 11 buttons and loops; at the waist there are eight hooks and eyes. The placket is 24 inches long, and has a pleat 3 inches wide, which covers the hooks. The dress is finished with a 1-1/2 inch deep machine stitched hem and is 146 inches in circumference at the bottom. The length is 55 inches from the neckline.

Fancy Little Girl's Slip
American, circa 1900

It is amazing to me how much time, love and money the Victorians put into slips for their little girl's dresses. Actually a baby slip is one of the simplest and sweetest of heirlooms to make.

This simple white batiste slip makes use of a fancy band, one of my favorite heirloom

A baby slip is one of the simplest and sweetest of heirlooms to make.

treatments. This one is particularly ornate for a slip and may have matched the dress. The band, a row of 5/8 inch wide insertion, a section of tucks and a row of gathered 1-1/4 inch wide edging was applied to the skirt just below a section of four 1/8 inch wide tucks.

A softly gathered French edging trims the neckline. It was tucked slightly under the hemmed edge and straight stitched on. The armholes were simply turned under, hemmed and left unadorned. A deep, 1-inch hand-stitched grow tuck was factored into the bodice of the slip. It would have added 2 inches to the length if it were taken out. Children tend to grow up before they grow out in the bodice area, so a slip with a grow tuck could fit for several years.

The back opening of this slip is 9 inches long and is closed with two buttons and buttonholes —one at the neckline and one at the bottom of the bodice. There is also an inside facing at the bottom of the bodice that measures 1 inch wide. My guess would be that this fabric was added for strength to a slip that would be worn for many years. The circumference of the slip is 52 inches. The inside seams are regular, unfinished edge seams, not French, with the exception of the tiny shoulder seams, which are flat felled.

Shark's Teeth Petticoat
American, circa 1900-1920

A friend and fellow antique-lover, Joann Cataldo, spotted this beauty in a Pratt Avenue antique store in my home town of Huntsville, Alabama. I rushed to the store following her phone call, and found the petticoat hanging so high that my first challenge was simply to get it down. I bought it without hesitation, but I didn't have it in my possession long, because I immediately sent it off to Sue Pennington Stewart with complete confidence that she could re-create the technique for today's heirloom sewing enthusiasts. We call this Shark's Teeth, and it has become one of our most popular techniques.

The petticoat features two sets of Shark's Teeth alternating between 3/4 inch wide row of Swiss embroidered insertion. Each section of Shark's Teeth is 3-1/2 inches deep. Swiss edging serves as the hemline. All of the pieces were joined together by flat felled seams. The waistband, which is 1-1/2 inches wide, closes with a button and buttonhole. The petticoat measures 14 inches from the top of the waistband to the bottom of the edging. The circumference of the skirt is 59 inches. The inside seams are French.

A Shark's Teeth measuring guide is included in the Martha Pullen Company catalogue and on the website for reproducing this technique. Complete Shark's Teeth instructions and a Shark's Teeth christening gown design can be found in the book *Grandmother's Hope Chest* from Martha Pullen Company.

Round Yoke Double Faggotted Blouse

French, circa 1900

This white batiste and lace French blouse was unearthed at a very nice antique store at the Paris Flea Market. Don't let the term "Flea Market" mislead you. I have seen $50,000 pieces of porcelain and $35,000 pieces of furniture at some of the more than 3000 shops. Merchandise and pricing truly runs the gamut.

This blouse was a little on the pricey side – not in the thousands mind you – but work like this rarely comes at a bargain. I simply couldn't resist it. The neckline and yoke are an all-in-one funnel treatment created with 15 strips of bias batiste that are 3/8 inch wide and separated by 1/4 inch precisely placed faggoting stitches. Entredeux finishes the bottom and serves to attach the yoke to the body of the blouse.

Four 3-inch long stays hold the collar in place. A 3-inch collar was very typical of blouses of this era. A swanlike neck was desirable, so clothing, however uncomfortable, was designed to enhance that feature. Every inch of this blouse was stitched by hand, including the tucks and inside seams, which are French.

The front of the blouse features four sets of five tucks run vertically from the yoke to the hem with three strips of beautiful lace inserted in between each tucked strip. The upper portion of the puffed sleeves has two sets of three tucks run horizontally with two pieces of the beautiful lace joined together in between. The sleeve is tucked vertically, from approximately the elbow down to the cuff, with four sets of five released tucks folded 1/8 inch wide and placed 1/8 inch apart. They measure 8 inches long from the "elbow" to the bottom of the cuff, which leads me to believe this blouse was originally made for a very tall woman.

Two pieces of lace joined together form the cuff. The ends were turned back and hemmed before four buttons and loops were added as a closure. In all, the sleeves are quite long, approximately 29 inches, so they would have puffed beautifully over the deep cuff, even on a tall woman.

I believe the lace, a single design and width used throughout, is a machine made version of a lace like "Point Colbert," which was heavier in style than some of the laces of the day and was traditionally finished along the edges with a picot. My research indicates that this "Point Colbert" lace became very popular in the late 1880s and remained popular until the early part of the 20th century. It was used in home décor as well as in clothing.

The back of the blouse has two sets of five tucks on either side of the center. The collar has eight buttons and button loops. The blouse has five covered buttonholes and five buttons. The buttonhole placket is made with four released tucks folded 1/8 inch wide, and placed 1/8 inch apart. The bottom of the blouse is finished with a double turned up narrow hem measuring 1/4 inch wide, caught up with a tiny running stitch.

French Silk Christening Ensemble
French, circa 1900

I truly believe this ecru silk christening ensemble is an international treasure, because it's virtually impossible to find all three pieces of a christening set still together after so many years. When I saw this three-piece christening ensemble in the Paris Flea Market, it was all I could do not to yell, "Sold!" without even asking the price or doing the usual bargaining. Although there are a number of flea markets in Paris, my favorite and by far the largest, is the Puces De St-Ouen also called the Porte de Clignancourt. This market is similar to antique malls and has, for the most part, very high-end goods. It houses 2-3,000 vendors, and it is open Saturday and Sunday.

The dress and coat I netted from my visit that day were made completely by hand -- the construction as well as the embroidery. Interestingly enough, the bonnet was made with some machine stitching, although the padded embroidery stitching was worked by hand. The design of the long-sleeve coat incorporates a capelet about the shoulders. It almost appears as if the two layers were smocked together; they were not.

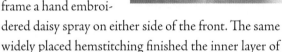

Five rows of double gathers create a beautiful rouching effect. The spaces between the rows of rouching measure 1/4 inch. The deep 2 inch wide hem on the caplet was stitched with hand hemstitching, creating a border to frame a hand embroidered daisy spray on either side of the front. The same widely placed hemstitching finished the inner layer of the cape, crossing at the inside bottom edges to form a decorative geometry. The entire inside seams were finished in the French style. The gathered yoke of the coat closes with three buttons and button loops. Narrow bias tubing of a self-fabric was used to fashion an elegant bow and streamers on the upper right side of the opening. The sleeves of

the coat were finished with a turned up 1-1/2 inch wide cuff. The coat is 26 inches long; the cape is 15-1/2 inches long.

Like the cape, the dress, a bishop style, was designed with five rows of rouching, but above that treatment, was added a bias binding followed by three rows of bias tubing attached with hand faggoting. The puffed short sleeves were also finished in a bias binding before the attachment of a single piece of bias tubing with hand faggoting. The back closure is simply a set of three pearl buttons and button loops. The hem of the dress, like the cape was secured with a 2 inch wide hand hemstitched hem. The embroidery on the front of the dress closely resembles that of the coat except for a ribbon interwoven throughout the daisy spray. The handwork embroidery is

a padded satin stitch, stem stitch, and French knots worked in ecru cotton floss. The length of the dress is 25 inches.

I can offer no explanation as to why part of the bonnet was sewn by machine. It could have been matter of saving time. Perhaps the seamstress felt it would be the one piece that might withstand the generations. I can only surmise. I do know that it is a very sweet style, with the headpiece constructed in three strips of fabric running from the back to the front. The beautifully embroidered brim runs perpendicular to the headpiece, and a wide silk ribbon was worn fashioned in a bow beneath the child's chin. The brim at its widest point is nearly 2 inches wide, the ties are 23 inches long, and the bonnet is fully lined.

A Baby's Hands

"Like crumpled blossom petals, moving slowly,

Upon the wind's frail, sighing lullaby;

And yet as high and wonderful and holy,

As God's great love that reaches from the sky!

As helpless as a bit of thistle blowing,

Across a meadow filled with lovely things,

And yet as strong-and subtle and as glowing,

As a white bird that flies on golden wings...

A baby's hands-weak, tiny fingers, groping

To find a place of tenderness and rest

They are the answer to the wistful hoping,

The prayer that lives in every woman's breast

A baby's hands-as shy as April weather,

Yet strong enough to hold the world together".

—Margaret Sangster, *The Delineator*, October, 1926

$\mathcal{L}$ily of the Valley White Coat
American, circa 1910

As a child, I remember always having an Easter or spring coat. Few adhere to this tradition any longer, which is really quite a shame. My coats were all lovely and very special, and I looked forward to them, even the hand-me-downs. That, combined with my special fondness for lily of the valley, compelled me to buy this vintage coat when I spotted it at an antique show in Massachusetts. I loved it so much; I didn't

even bother to haggle—much. I knew I would be taking it home at any price.

This coat was made of a heavy white piqué, one of my favorite fabrics. All of the embroidery was worked by hand. The large shawl collar is detailed with padded satin stitch sprigs of lily of the valley with hand embroidered ribbons tying the flowers at various points. A larger sprig of lily of the valley tied with a bow lends interest to the back of the collar. The two front points of the collar fasten to the coat with snaps to keep the collar neatly in place. The collar is 10 inches wide; the coat is 23 inches long. The circumference of the coat is 52 inches.

There is story behind the hem of the coat. Upon closer examination of the hem, I could tell that it had

been let out, so that a child could wear it for yet one more season. On the inside, the story unfolded more distinctly. A piece of cotton broadcloth was added to the bottom of the coat to face the hem on the inside and squeeze out every bit of useable length. The hem was put into place with a straight machine stitch.

The dropped band on the coat is 3-1/2 inches wide and is embellished with very simple satin stitch embroidery It also closes securely with two buttons and buttonholes. The sleeves are quite fascinating, in particular, the sleeve cuffs, which have a turned back scalloped edge and were beautifully embroidered with lily of the valley sprigs. French seams were used exclusively in this coat including the ones to insert the sleeves. It is a masterpiece of workmanship. The coat closes with handmade buttonholes and beautiful crocheted covered ball buttons.

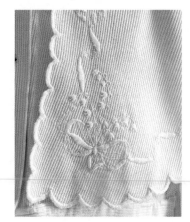

English Embroidered Motif Woman's Dress

English, circa 1895

This piece is in remarkably good condition indicating it was worn sparingly. The high, 3-inch wide waistband is embellished all the way around with 1/8-inch vertical tucks placed 1/2 inch apart; these were sewn in by machine. Outlining the tucked panel on top and bottom of the tucked section is a 7/8-inch wide piece of insertion, which was topstitched by machine.

The bodice section is quite elaborate and is made up of two layers. The main bodice has the fullness gathered

with several tiny tucks in the center. The neckline is squared off with two rows of mitered insertion. Two additional rows topstitched horizontally fill in the neckline. A decorative motif was tacked on by hand at the center of the bodice. The top layer of the bodice is somewhat like the "modern" version of a late 17th century fichu. The 4-inch wide panels are a combination of batiste, insertion, and slightly gathered edging. They were attached under the waistband in the front and back and go over the shoulder where they were tacked by hand to secure. This fichu-like treatment adds dimension to the upper portion of the gown. The 3/4-length sleeves were slightly gathered at the shoulder and consist of batiste, insertion, and gathered edging, a treatment repeated three times then a section of batiste and a fancy band of two rows

of insertion and edging. All the lace work was overlapped and topstitched by machine.

The back of the dress is similar to the front, although four rows of insertion fill in the neckline instead of two. A medallion was also tacked to the center back, however because it falls on top of the back placket one assumes it was tacked on the left side of the garment and attached with hooks on the right side. Hooks and eyes are no longer found on the medallion but they do attach the lace portion of the back closing; pearl buttons and handmade buttonholes close the rest of the gown.

The skirt of this gown has some slight fullness gathered by 1/16 inch tucks sewn down about 5 inches and placed 3/4 inch apart, except for the two tucks right and left of center, which were placed 1-5/8 inch apart. Ten inches down from the waistband starts the decorative work on the skirt —a row of insertion, a 5-inch panel with three 1/2-inch horizontal tucks in the center, placed 7/8 inch apart. This repeats four times, which left about 6-1/4 inches of fabric, 2-1/4 inches of which was turned under and machine hemmed. Raw seams were left on the inside of the skirt. The length of the dress from shoulder to hem is approximately 53 inches.

White Work Leaves & Bows Baby's Dress
American, circa 1910-1930

The White Work Leaves and Bows dress came from Puyallup, Washington. It is a high yoke baby dress made of a medium weight 100 percent cotton fabric. The measurements of the neckline and the sleeves lead me to believe it was originally constructed for a very tiny baby. The neckline, measures 9 inches in circumference, only 8 inches when buttoned. The sleeves are a scant 4 inches around—only a tiny baby's hand would fit through such a small opening.

The bodice was finished with a bias binding, which is 1/4 inch wide; pretty hand crocheted lace adorns the neckline and the sleeve cuff. A very sweet gathered ruffle edged in crochet trim outlines the square yoke in front and back, running from center back over the shoulders and around the front of the yoke. The finished width of the ruffle with the trim is 1 inch. The ruffle was hemmed in the interior edge, gathered and straight stitched to the yoke of the garment leaving a little folded-over edge exposed—not encased in the dress seam. The ruffle was gathered in a 2-to-1 fullness.

The elegant white work embroidery on the bodice and skirt is a simple branch and bow design worked in a circular fashion. Two motifs embellish the yoke and were placed 1-1/4 inch apart. There are ten motifs worked around the skirt hem and placed approximately 3-3/4 inches apart.

The side seams of the dress are French; the rest of the seams were simply straight stitched and left unfinished. The 2-inch hem was stitched by machine. The dress is 31 inches long. The skirt circumference is 62 inches. The back opening including the skirt placket is 10 inches. There are three tiny buttonholes and buttons on the back of the yoke.

Embroideries for little people tempt us more than almost any other needlework, partly because of the appeal of childhood and not a bit less because of the attraction of childish designs.

—*Modern Priscilla*, 1915

$\mathscr{S}$wiss Embroidery "K" Combing Coat

American, circa 1900

This beautiful combing coat is a perfect example of the interest in women's lingerie, which abounded around 1900. The following ideas come from the June, 1903 edition of *The Delineator*: *"Where is the woman who does not love dainty lingerie? The feeling is inborn, and while the desire to be prettily gowned is uppermost with many women, it may safely be said that, given a choice the majority would favor a collection of pretty and dainty lingerie in preference to numerous and elaborate gowns. By this it need not be inferred that all attention should be given the underlinen, and little or no care expended upon the outer garments. A fitting amount of both time and money should be expended upon each, so that in one's own wardrobe, from beginning to end; there will be a conformity of materials and trimmings which is consistent with good taste."*

This beautifully constructed white batiste and linen combing coat, which I purchased in Massachusetts, offers some magnificent details. What is a combing coat? Victorian woman wore a combing coat while they were styling their hair in order not to get hair on their undergarments or dress. This particular piece was constructed both by hand and machine. Underneath the magnificent collar are two sets of six 1/4-inch tucks spaced 1/4 inch apart in the front and two sets of four tucks 3/8 inches wide in back to control the fullness in the yoke area. The tucks were sewn by machine.

The coat was made from a very fine grade of handkerchief linen; the collar was made from batiste and Swiss trims. The collar is two pieces of Swiss trim joined with Swiss entreduex. Both sides of the Swiss trim—straight and gathered—were attached to the entredeux by hand. The total back length of the V collar is 12-1/2 inches. The total back length of the combing coat is 24 inches.

The front placket is flanked with Swiss entredeux on both sides. Swiss entreduex also secures the 1-1/4-inch wide hem. The coat closes with four buttons and four buttonholes.

The magnificent puffed sleeves blossom with fullness at the bottom and were hand rolled and whipped to what I call a fancy band. The band consists of a piece of Swiss entredeux, 5/8 inches of French insertion, a 3/4 inch wide piece of Swiss batiste, another piece of French insertion, Swiss entredeux, and finally a 4-3/8 inch width of Swiss edging gathered, hand rolled, and whipped to the bottom edge of a pretty flounce.

The special surprise for me when I found this piece was the hand monogrammed "K" at the bottom right-hand corner of the coat. It was placed 2-1/2 inches from the outside front edge of the coat and 3 inches from the bottom edge. The Victorians, like elegantly dressed women today, loved monograms. How I wish I knew more about the person who belonged to that initial "K."

Tucks, Glorious Tucks Christening Dress
American, circa 1880

Just how wonderful can a christening dress be? I believe this piece answers that question. The tucks alone simply take my breath away. The dress is quite old. The decorative V insert at the neckline was Swiss made specifically for a christening dress. One clue lies in the very point of the Swiss insert that overlaps the bodice-to-skirt join. I have been told that for a baby girl's christening that point would have been tucked under. The work on the insert resembles Ayrshire embroidery, although it was made on a Swiss machine. The matching V edging running along the central piece was also made specifically for this dress. I believe that the unusual sleeves—a straight Swiss piece stitched down on top of a main sleeve Swiss piece—were woven for this particular dress.

The neck casing, which has Swiss edging around the top, is run with a very fine cotton drawstring to draw up the dress to fit different size babies. A coordinating narrow Swiss trim embellishes the seam where the bodice joins the skirt.

The skirt was made of heavier batiste than the top. The design in the Swiss edging around the bottom of the skirt does not match the trim on the rest of the gown. There are 65 tucks on the skirt of this dress, which would have taken a seamstress hours to mark and stitch perfectly straight. The tucks are nearly 1/4 inch wide with 1/8 inch between each tuck. The dress is 38 inches long, and the circumference is 78 inches.

Since scooped neck style Christening dresses closed with a drawstring at the neck and waist, additional closures needed to be applied down the back opening. Some of my dresses have buttons and buttonholes; others were secured with tiny beauty pins. These little pins were generally decorative in nature, and because they were so small, it is rare to find a matching set of them. Occasionally you will find two or three antique baby pins at a flea market or antique shop that have been connected through the decades by a chain.

Drawn Thread Woman's Blouse
American, circa 1900

There are several reasons I purchased this blouse in a little antique shop in Pensacola, Florida. The most obvious reason is that it's simply beautiful, and it could be recreated today by anyone skilled in the art of pulled thread stitches. The pulled thread designs bloom in a variety of patterns and were worked on the basic bodice from the shoulder seams to the bottom of the blouse. On the blouse, underneath the inner, pulled thread L-shapes, are two 1/2 inch wide tucks with a motif of drawn thread buttonholes stitched on top. It is shaped like a triangle with little Vs on the bottom, six in all.

The perfectly plain sleeves are slightly gathered at the shoulder line. The bottom of the 1-3/4 inch long cuff closes with two buttons and two buttonholes. The sleeve placket is 7 inches long. The front placket of the blouse is 1-1/2 inches wide.

The back is embellished with four 1/2 inch wide tucks. Upon looking at this blouse initially, I thought it was made with a short collar; it only measures 1 inch wide. Actually part of the embellishment is missing. Three buttonholes on the collar indicate that a gathered flounce or collar embellishment would have buttoned to the short collar.

The current buttons are not original to this blouse. The two top buttons were stitched on after the two buttonholes were stitched shut. These buttons are not true to the period in which this blouse was originally made.

Although the buttons might indicate the blouse was not as old as originally estimated, I have my reasons for dating it from the early part of the 1900s. The blouse fullness was stabilized with a waist tape, which gathered the blouse in, evenly to the 26-inch waistline. Another reason is that when I buttoned the blouse with its modern buttons, I discovered that it was in the pigeon breast style, which was prominent around the turn of the 20th century. I can't be sure as to what year the gold and pearl buttons were added—a typical variety purchased at a fabric store within the last 50 years —but I'm encouraged that someone actually wore this gorgeous piece and was creative enough to fix it the best way she knew how.

Oval Yoke Embroidery and Tucks Baby Dress
English, circa 1910

I purchased this little white batiste dress one cold morning at Bermondsey. It was far from perfect in condition, but the beauty and sewing details of the dress totally enchanted me. What struck me first, was the embroidered piece in front, which is Swiss made. How do I know this? To determine if antique embroidery were handmade or manufactured in Switzerland, turn the piece to the back. Find matching motifs. Do the threads cross at the same place on the matching motifs? If so, then the piece was Swiss or machine made. If the crossing threads don't match, then it was most likely made by hand.

Frequently, around the turn of the last century, pieces of Swiss embroidery were made specifically to be inserted in children's and adult's garments. This particular piece of embroidery is an exquisite example. It was woven with flowers, drawn thread (by machine) centers for two of the flowers, and a drawn thread oval with padded satin stitch flowers on top of the machine drawn work in the bottom oval. A tiny little cross can be found at the center of the central flower and French lace was inserted in the middle of the large drawn thread oval.

The front of the dress has eight released tucks on either side of the panel. Construction of a dress like this would involve fashioning released tucks as far across a batiste panel as necessary to accommodate the embroidered piece. Two of the released tucks on the antique piece are barely visible since the oval lace motif covers most of them. The tucks were folded 1/8 inch wide and spaced a scant 1/4 inch apart.

Swiss entredeux was used in the shoulder seams, to join the embroidered piece to the dress, to attach the sleeves to the dress and to ready the neckline for lace attachment. The application of entredeux at the neckline and around the sleeves was rather unusual. Both seam allowances of the entredeux were left intact. They were simply turned under and straight stitched; gathered French lace edging was then stitched to the top finished seam allowance of the entredeux. The sleeves were finished in the same manner.

The back of the dress has 13 released tucks on either side of the opening, the same size and placement as the front tucks.

The ruffle on the bottom of the dress measures 3-3/4 inches including the 1-inch French lace edging, which is a lovely flower and dot pattern. The ruffle was attached to the bottom of the dress with Swiss entredeux. Another interesting sewing technique was used to attach the French lace at the bottom of the ruffle. The ruffle was hemmed with a 1/4 inch wide hem and straight stitched by machine. The French lace edging was simply straight stitched on top of the finished hem.

The back of the dress closes with four tiny buttons and buttonholes. The back opening of the dress measures 8-1/2 inches long. The circumference of the bottom of the dress is 48 inches. French seams were used for the side seams. Remember, the fullness is mostly from the released tucks on both the front and back of the dress; however, this dress has an interesting twist. There is a hidden pleat adding extra fullness underneath each sleeve. These underarm pleats add nearly 4 inches extra to each side.

Every mother likes to see her little one daintily garbed, and who can blame her? She delights, too, in having all baby's belongings as fine and pretty as possible. Perhaps there is nothing in which she takes more pride than the neatly fitted carriage in which the wee king or queen of the household takes a daily outing; it sends a flush of pleasure to her cheek to see passers-by glance at the little vehicle, then turn to look again with a smile that betokens admiration.

—Addie May Bodwell for *Needlecraft Magazine*, October, 1913

Always thread the needle from the end that hangs from the spool, thus working with the twist of the thread, so that knots and kinks will be avoided. A broken thread twists better to a point than a cut one; but always cut your thread when you finish your work. You cannot break it off close enough to the material without pulling the stitching out of shape.

—A Few Secrets of Successful Sewing, Mrs. M.V.H.
Illustrated Needlework, May, 1923

Netting Dress with Blue Embroidery
American, circa 1910

To be truthful, I don't remember where I purchased this dress, but I believe it was in Massachusetts many years ago. It's unusual to find a dress from this era with any color on it, so what I do remember is snatching it up quickly.

The embroidery is not only blue, it is almost navy blue. Both the bodice and collar are half cotton netting and half Swiss organdy over which the shadow-embroidered flowers were worked. Hemstitching was worked solely on the organdy and was even used to close the sleeve seams.

There are no side seams on the bodice, which measures 32 inches finished. The seamstress either used very wide organdy or ran the organdy lengthwise. The organdy portion of the bodice begins at the five rows of blue hemstitching. The splashes of hand embroidery hold much of this dress's charm. The seamstress worked shadow stitching and handmade eyelets in groupings on the bodice, skirt and the collar. She trimmed the 3 inch wide belt with what can be best described as an uneven, hand stitched zigzag.

The collar is permanently attached on one side from the center front around to the back opening. The collar snaps in place on the other side around the neck edging. Once the dress was on and closed in the back, the collar was brought around and snapped in place, as shown left. The seamless collar covers the opening in the back, and from the front, the snaps are hidden.

Like the bodice and collar of the dress, the sleeves were cut from two fabrics; the bottom quarter is organdy, the remainder is netting. Blue hemstitching again serves to camouflage the join. The seamstress carried this same design element through to the skirt, on which the two fabrics are joined by a set of five rows of hemstitching. A second set of five hemstitched rows was worked 5 inches beneath the first. A 3 inch wide hem was hand sewn with running stitches.

A netting underskirt trimmed with eight rows of organdy ruffles not only lends fullness to dress, it adds a decorative element, as the pretty organdy ruffles show through the sheer outer netting. The netting under dress closes in the back with metal snaps; the dress closes with metal hooks and eyes. Even with the added layers of netting, the see-through dress would have required a full slip underneath. This dress is slightly larger than most in my collection with a waistline that measures 28 inches. The finished back length is 49 inches.

French Boudoir Pillow
French, circa 1900

It probably won't surprise you to learn that my French Boudoir Pillow came from the Paris Flea Market. It was in a remote booth and one of the fruits of my "just one more booth" antiquing philosophy.

The pillow was embroidered and constructed by hand. The fabric is a bridal white organdy. The handwork is cutwork intermingled with padded satin stitch flower sprays that almost completely cover the piece. The pillow without the ruffle measures 23-1/2 inches by 18 inches. The ruffle is 3-1/2 inches wide with a 1/2 inch wide lace edging. It is also detailed with a delicate drawn threadwork path. A 1-1/4 inch wide silk ribbon is run through buttonholes all around the outside of the pillow, and large bows are tied at each corner. The silk ribbon is very worn, but I chose not to replace it since it is rare to find a piece with the original ribbon. The buttonholes are 1/2 inch wide and spaced 1-1/4 inches apart; they run parallel to the pillow seam and are 1/4 inch away from the seam. The pillow is lined with a robin's egg blue silk fabric, and there is even an under ruffle of this same silk. Interestingly enough, the underlined ruffle is not hemmed; it appears to have been cut with pinking scissors that left a scalloped raw edge.

Boy's Linen Suit
English, circa 1915

I found this suit early one Saturday morning at the "mall" along Portobello Road. It's rare to find boy's clothing. Having raised four boys, I imagine it's because boys wore out their clothing. And just as today, boys probably had fewer outfits. This particular oatmeal-colored suit has weathered the years well, primarily because it was made of a very heavy linen. It is so heavy, in fact, that it would have been rough against the skin, which could be another reason it has survived; I can imagine a mother meeting with quite a protest when she asked her little boy to wear it.

Two other fabrics were used in a combination with the oatmeal-colored linen: a softer fabric of an oatmeal-color with orange and blue stripes for the collar, and yet a third texture of an oatmeal-based fabric woven with black threads was used for the pants.

An opening for "bathroom purposes" was fashioned into the front of the pants. This was a typical and practical feature on boy's apparel. Larger suits might have had buttons for a closure, but this suit is approximately a size 5, and it would have been difficult for such a young child to manipulate the buttons. Later on, of course, zippers would have been used.

The collar was cut as a sailor collar in front, but was rounded in back. The width of the back collar is 3-3/4 inches. The sleeves measure 9-1/2 inches long, which would have made them 3/4-length on a child. The shirt pockets have a flap closed with a button and buttonhole. The pants also have pockets, a popular feature that has endured in boy's clothing. Although the belt is missing, the suit was constructed with tailored belt loops made from the pants fabric. There are five belt loops in all, two on the front, and three in back. The total length of the suit is 27-1/4 inches.

Normally, a linen garment made with short pants, would have been worn during the spring or summer months, but because the linen is so heavy and younger boys wore short pants year round, I can't say definitively that this is the case. Traditionally, however, boy's suits for the winter were made with long pants and sleeves and often cut from wool, a fabric we would most likely use as a blend and only for boy's dress clothing today.

This garment was completely machine made with the exception of the buttonholes; the inside seams are flat felled, and it is overall a beautifully constructed garment.

> This suit is well made, even giving a little boy lots of pockets, something all little boys love.

$\mathcal{P}$ink Bow Ruffle Dress
French, circa 1910-1930

Of all the pieces in my collection, this white baby dress is one of a handful I know to have been originally commissioned or store bought. The most obvious clue is the little tag in the back that reads "L. Rouff-Rue Royale, Paris." The tag, which is as elegant as the garment, is white with very pale silver lettering making it nearly invisible. In my imagination, this sweet little dress was purchased for a child's second birthday party; in reality, big bows were sometimes incorporated into a dress design to mark a birthday girl's big day.

The dress is batiste garnished with tucks, French lace, and a pink oversized silk satin bow stitched to the neckline above each shoulder. The width of the silk satin ribbon is 2 inches. The total length of each tied bow is 8 inches; the length of each tail is 3-1/2 inches. The densely woven design on the round thread lace makes it a heavier, less airy trim. Although the child who wore this dress may have been too young to have a favorite color, pink has always been the most popular hue to lend to little girl's clothing. She may have worn the dress for her 2-year-old portrait with a pink or white slip worn beneath —either would have been beautiful.

Underneath the very wide ruffle collar, 30 released tucks folded 1/8 inch wide and spaced 1/4 inch apart contain the fullness in front. Fifteen are spaced on either side in the back. The front neck ruffle is 30 inches around and 6-1/4 inches deep. It was trimmed with wide insertion lace two-thirds of the way down and finished with a 3/8 inch wide edging applied straight. The ruffle is split on each shoulder and in the back to accommodate three buttons, button loops and an 8-inch long placket. The back neck ruffle is 15 inches on each side. The buttons are closely spaced, only about 1/2 inch apart down the back opening. The neckline was finished with a bias binding, which houses a cotton drawstring to adjust the dress to the child. Entredeux was applied to the binding finish to serve as a bridge between the binding and the neck ruffle.

The beautiful straight sleeves were inserted into the dress with Swiss entredeux. They were trimmed with the same French insertion and edging as was used on the neckline ruffle. The skirt is a lovely combination of tucks and a single strip of the wide round thread insertion. The 1/16 inch wide tucks were applied first in a group of two 7-1/2 inches down from the neckline, skipping 1-1/2 inches and applying a group of 3 tucks, then the insertion, three more tucks, and finally four tucks before finishing with a 1-1/2 inch wide machine stitched hem. The circumference of the dress is 46 inches.

French Silk Negligee
French, circa 1915

Lingerie and foundations, by far, are one of the most interesting categories of women's apparel. What the fairer sex has subjected itself to in the name of beauty has been nothing short of barbaric. Pulling corsets so tight that they interfered with breathing, for instance, was an accepted mode of behavior for most of the 19th century and into the next.

By 1900, women's intimate apparel was being openly advertised in catalogs and magazines. The following quote is from *Needlecraft*, February, 1917: *"The Alluring Negligee: There is never a girl or woman who does not delight in a dainty negligee, with cap to match. Indeed, such alluring feminine apparel is now considered quite an indispensable part of every woman's wardrobe."*

I purchased this ecru silk negligee at the Paris Flea Market. The silk is very thin, but not as thin as China silk. As is true of most of my silk pieces, it is not in the best of repair. Silk simply does not hold up through the years like cotton or linen. The condition of the silk simply became a non-issue when I realized how many yards of exquisite French lace were used to embellish this negligee. The lacework is simply breathtaking.

The detailed sewing begins at the shoulder of this garment where a long panel of pintucked silk is flanked by pieces of French insertion. The pintucks are 1/16 inch wide with 1/16 inch between. The entire pintucked piece is only 3/4 inch wide. The French insertion is also 3/4 inch wide. A 2 inch wide piece of insertion runs around this strip and is mitered at the bottom corners. Diagonal strips of ecru silk with French insertion between them are positioned at the outside edges of pintucked strip. The silk strips are 2 inches wide and the French insertion is 3/4 inches wide. On the inside of the pintucked piece is a 1-3/4 inch wide piece of French insertion, which travels to the bottom of the gown and pours into a glorious piece of French edging. This 4 inch wide edging is slightly gathered down the front before curving around into the bottom treatment. A piece of 3/4 inch wide French insertion serves as the "side seam" of the robe. The back of the negligee repeats the front detailing.

The collar is a beautifully shaped sailor style, which is squared in the back. It is composed entirely of French laces and framed all the way around with the same beautiful 4 inch wide slightly gathered edging as runs down the front and around the hemline. The collar is 10 inches long in the back.

The fancy band of this negligee is 25 inches long and has fabulous details of released tucks 3 inches long in sets of six around the top of the fancy band. Little columns of French insertion separate the sets of tucks. These columns of 5/8 inch wide French insertion are 4-1/2 inches long and are pointed at the ends. The next row of embellishment is made from more 5/8 inch wide insertion mitered into square shapes around the skirt. The width of the top horizontal piece of French insertion in this squared shape is 3 inches; it is 2-1/2 inches from top to bottom, vertically; and the bottom horizontal piece of French insertion is 4-3/8 inches wide. All of the corners are mitered.

Nine-1/2 inches from the top of the fancy band is a piece of 5/8 inch wide French insertion going the full width of the fancy band. Below this horizontal piece of insertion is another silk piece 2-1/4 inches wide with two 1/4 inch folded tucks spaced 1/4 inch apart. Another piece of 5/8 inch wide French lace insertion is beneath. The gathered ruffle of the fancy band was also made up of several beautiful sections. The first is a 4 inch wide silk band, which has three folded 1/4 inch wide tucks near the bottom. The next piece is of 2-1/8 inches wide French insertion followed by a slightly gathered band of 2-1/4 inch wide silk. The bottom lace is the 4 inch wide edging that is consistently used throughout. The total back length of the negligee is 50 inches.

Although I might actually wear a magnificent negligee like this today, I would more likely pour this much work into the skirt of a christening gown, where these techniques would last for generations.

There is never a girl or woman who does not delight in a dainty negligee...

—*Needlecraft*, February, 1917

Square Neck Pinafore
American, circa 1900

What could be sweeter than a little girl in a pinafore? This pinafore made of linen and Swiss embroideries is simple, yet elegant. Linen is a heavier material and would have held up well in the wash since pinafores frequently covered other dresses to keep them clean. Today, we refer to imported cotton trim as Swiss embroideries; however in the April, 1914 issue of *Needlecraft*, Swiss embroideries were referred to as "embroidered flouncing."

The front of this pinafore was constructed with two sets of five 1/8-inch tucks spaced 1/4 inch apart. The flounce or Swiss embroidered insertions on the skirt were applied with entredeux on either side; they are 2 inches wide. The shoulders were made of embroidered edging as were the ruffles over the arms. Two rows of Swiss insertion were added on either side of the sets of center tucks.

The back was made to incorporate two sets of four tucks and closes with two buttons. One button fastens with a loop, the other with a buttonhole. Nearly the entire back remains open where the under dress would have shown. The circumference of this little pinafore is 45 inches. The pretty Swiss insertion or flouncing ruffle was slightly gathered before applying it to finish the bottom. The lace on the pinafore is called chemical lace and was quite the fashion starting in the 1880s when the machine embroidery manufacturers in Switzerland began to make chemical lace to imitate needlepoint lace.

Pinafores were worn to protect clothing, and I thought this paragraph charming from *The Delineator*, February, 1902. It specifically addresses children's play for which this type of pinafore was designed: *"Too often the fond parent feels that the dress makes the child, and consequently adorns it in the latest and showiest fashion without realizing that harm instead of good is done to the child by either hampering its action or making it over conscious. The everyday child will revel in dirt. It accumulates it by satisfying its curiosity, for its hands are into everything as well as its feet and knees and clothes. The child must get near mother earth. Mothers should encourage the mud pie making and sand digging for the little human plant, and the dress and clothing should be such that the child should not be reproved for muddy shoes, soiled and torn dresses. If the child is persuaded that his righteousness will be established and the approval of his dear mother will be obtained by keeping clean he will do so; he can be trained to it, but it will be at the expenses of the freedom of his muscles."*

The Claudia Nightdress
American, circa 1915

It is exceedingly difficult to try to explain what I look for at a show such as the one I frequent every other year in Massachusetts. Basically, I collect white clothes of almost every variety and the occasional linen. A few years ago, I became fascinated with "clothes which speak" or "linens which speak"—my favorite way to describe antique pieces that have words written on them. As I made my first, very quick run through this huge show, I looked, as I always do, through the women's lingerie racks in each booth. At first, I passed right over this white batiste nightdress, but then I paused, realizing I had seen some letters right underneath the puffing and lace. The tiny, hand embroidered letters spelled "Claudia." Even tinier French knots and one lone bullion rose garnished the satin stitched, white-on-white lettering

Looking closer at the gown, I found that the shoulder straps as well as the top of the front and back of the gown were made from 1 inch wide puffing strips. Tiny white entredeux was applied on either side of this puffing. Slightly gathered 1/2 inch wide, white French round thread lace (heavier lace) was used to trim the neckline. This same entredeux and slightly gathered French lace treatment was used to encircle the arm openings.

The fullness in the back was controlled by a series of 14 released tucks folded 1/8 inch wide, the longest of which at center back measures 6-1/2 inches. The tucks are divided in half, each facing the middle. Tucks are stitched down the front of the gown—eight sets of three released tucks. The center tuck in each set is 1/8 inch wide; the tucks on each side are 1/16 inch

wide. All of these front center released tuck groups are 1 inch long.

The front of the bodice also has a truly beautiful piece of 2 inch wide round thread lace stitched below the entredeux joining the bottom of the puffing and stitched on top of the tucked piece, which is the skirt.

The "Claudia" lettering is stitched on the left side of the gown right above the heart. The side seams are French and the straight hem was stitched with tiny whipstitches.

My truest guess would be that this was a trousseau gown for a bride named "Claudia." When I was in college, there was a shop in Birmingham called "The Trousseau Shop," which featured monogrammed lingerie for the bride and anyone else, of course, who could afford that kind of splendid undergarment. This tradition of monogramming with either letters or a name was also very prominent in Victorian times. Once at a Christie's auction, I passed up an undergarment that was hand embroidered with Queen Victoria's crest. Although I regret it to this day, it was simply too expensive, and I could not justify the cost. I was told at the auction, however, that Queen Victoria had all of her lingerie embroidered with her tiny royal crest, usually right above her heart on the left side, just like the placement of "Claudia."

Long Netting Lace Christening Cape
Australian, circa 1900

I have found some of my most beautiful netting garments in Australia on the few antiquing outings that I have been able to make while down under. The Long Netting Lace Christening Cape is one of them.

This cape is just that, a cape. It does not have a coat with sleeves underneath the top layer, as do some of my pieces. The fabric is one of the most beautiful, embroidered nettings I have come across. It suits the shape of the cape so perfectly, I'd like to believe it was pre-designed at the factory to use for a christening cape. I've also poured over this cape thinking that it quite possibly was hand embroidered with the lace tape that scrolls down both the cape and the over cape. It may have been a purchased kit of some kind, but I confess, its origin remains a mystery to me.

The total length of the cape is 35 inches. The length of the top cape is 15 inches. The cape has a silk lining, which is edged on the bottom and around the center front with tiny baby French edging. The silk lining has held up amazingly well over the years. Two narrow netting ruffles define the neckline; three rows of puffing start at the center neck on both the cape and capelet and continue down both fronts and curve around to finish the hem. This cape would be just as gorgeous for a christening today as it was more than a hundred years ago.

The comfortable cape is just

the thing for a baby's outing.

— *Modern Priscilla, July, 1922*

Entredeux Tucks Child's Middy Dress
American, circa 1910

I have always treasured this simple, white batiste dress. It's sole embellishment is the purchased French edging gathered around the neckline. It came to me from somewhat meager surroundings, stuffed into a bag in a vendor's booth on Pier 49 in New York City. Once I'd unearthed it, however, I couldn't let it go. While it seemed simple and not very exciting to most people, it held a world of sewing excitement for me.

This seamstress, I can imagine, had a hemstitching machine and loved to use it; it would have created a much more cost-efficient embellishment than rows of lace, and perhaps she simply didn't enjoy hand embroidery. The style of the dress, a middy, was quite popular around 1910.

On this particular example, tucks served not only as the primary form of embellishment, they acted as a foundation for hemstitching, which was run down the center of each one. To gather in the fullness of the dress and fashion a fitted yoke, nine 1/2 inch wide tucks positioned 3/8 inch apart made up the front of the middy. The centermost tuck from neck down measures 4-1/2 inches long. The effect was repeated on the back of the dress with four hemstitched tucks positioned on either side of the back opening. The two tucks that serve as a collar running around the neckline, were also secured with hemstitching, this time at the base of each tuck.

The sleeves are plain and simple. The 1 inch wide waistband was tucked twice, like the collar and hemstitched at the base of the tucks. Beneath the waistband, the gathered skirt was constructed with a large 1-1/2 inch wide tuck hemstitched at the base. The hem was folded equally deep and secured with hemstitching. An enclosed placket was designed to hide the four buttons and buttonholes, which fasten the dress in back. The inside seams of the dress are a combination of French and straight, unfinished seams. The finished back length of the dress is 21 inches.

> On this particular example, tucks served not only as the primary form of embellishment, but they also acted as a foundation for hemstitching.

Swiss Embroidery Motif on Organdy
Chrysanthemum & Leaves
Swiss, circa 1880

The first observation I can make about this gorgeous Swiss piece is that I am not sure it was intended to be a chrysanthemum at all. It's clearly a floral abstract, but I saw a chrysanthemum in my mind's eye, and thus it was named. The Swiss tried to make lace on their embroidery machines. They have produced netting since the 1800s, and, they also embroidered beautiful patterns on netting, which I refer to as Swiss lace. However, I believe this piece was embroidered on organdy, the fabric cut away and French lace added behind the cutwork sections. I do not claim to be a lace historian, although one day I would like to study this subject in great depth. My fascination for pieces such as this beautiful Swiss motif is in how it would have been used in Victorian clothing or in clothing or table linens for today's sewing enthusiast. The large quantities of Swiss embroideries and batiste garments that have survived over a century are a great testament to the quality of the products. The Swiss embroidery machines began production in the mid 1850s, and they are still running today.

The large quantities of Swiss embroideries and batiste garments that have survived over a century are a great testament to the quality of the products. Lace machinery was introduced into Switzerland by the 1850s; however embroidery machines continued to be the mechanism of choice in that country. Machine Swiss embroidery was a well-established industry in the St. Gallen region of Switzerland by the 1850s and continues today. Martha Pullen Company has always imported embroideries and Swiss batiste from this particular region of Switzerland.

Victorian Pintucks Dress
English, circa 1910

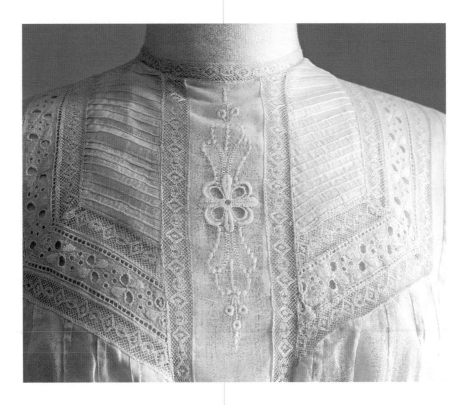

Despite the excessive trim, this white batiste and lace garment was intended as an afternoon dress. I found it at an outdoor dealer during one of my early morning trips to Bermondsey. Two features were most appealing to me; the pintucks placed in a diagonal fashion and the elegant white-on-white embroidery in three places on the dress.

Today, we are so fortunate to have double needles and pintuck feet to make large areas of pintucking a breeze. These pintucks were whipped by hand. They are very narrow and placed 1/8 inch apart. The elongated areas of white-on-white embroidery were actually pre-embroidered strips, which at the time were quite popular coming out of Switzerland.

The seamstress apparently had three strips that she incorporated magnificently into the design of her dress. The embroidery design incorporates cutwork in the middle and is white on white. On this dress, the Swiss strips were used at the center front of the bodice and as two long panels running down the sides of the skirt.

The Swiss strip on the bodice is flanked by pieces of French lace insertion. Next to this center panel on each side the seamstress mitered angles of French lace and Swiss insertion around an insert of pintucks. Entredeux was applied between the Swiss and French laces. The fabric fullness at the shoulders and below the lace work was controlled with a series of released tucks measuring 1/4 inch and spaced some distance apart. The stand-up collar is a simple circle of 1/2 inch wide French insertion.

The fitted sleeves are beautifully and simply embellished with two rows of French lace insertion running down the entire length to a finish of flat lace insertion.

A waistline was formed by two rows of French insertion at the top and bottom of an unadorned fabric strip. The skirt was beautifully made with four rows of folded 1/4 inch wide tucks at the center, flanked by two lengths of Swiss edging. This center panel runs to the hemline where it extends to a width of 9 inches. Because the Swiss embroidered panels were possibly too short to run the entire length of the skirt, the seamstress cleverly fashioned her design to make the most of her limitations. The side panels, which incorporate the Swiss pieces and the skirt as it continues around the back, are

18 inches shorter than the center panel. To make up the difference, the seamstress applied a gathered ruffle or fancy band around the skirt, which was attached to the insertion running along the sides of the center panel and to the bottom of the shorter portion of the skirt.

The panels next to the Swiss trim on the skirt carry through the decorative work of the bodice in long sections of angled pintucks, French insertion entredeux, and Swiss trims.

The fancy band/ruffle is 18 inches deep and features two sets of three 1/4 inch tucks and a 2 inch deep machine stitched hem.

The back of the dress has four sets of 3-1/4 inch wide tucks and a single strip of French lace on either side. The dress closes with four buttonholes and pearl buttons; the waistline is closed with hooks and eyes. There are no French seams on the inside of this dress.

This summer, I have six dresses instead of two—prettier dresses, more stylish and better made—and for the first time in my life, dresses that my friends say have my own individuality in every line.

—Ad from The Women's Institute in *Modern Priscilla*, 1922

Pin things together carefully, baste often, and press well. Do not cut the notches shown in the pattern. Even if the seams are so deep the material will not pull out, you may want to let out the seam sometime and the notch will prevent this.

—A Few Secrets to Successful Sewing,
Illustrated Needlework, May, 1923

French Puffing Dress
French, circa 1900

My pretty pink and white French Puffing Dress came from Lyon, France at the Villurbanne Flea Market. A student at one of my schools tipped me off to this flea market, and I booked a short trip to France for the sole purpose of antiquing there.

It was only after I made my reservations that I picked up a book about European flea markets. This is what I read: "The Villeurbanne flea market is one of the great junk markets of France and fun to visit, to boot, despite its unappealing setting. It can be tricky getting here; if you don't have a car, it is downright difficult, and even with a car you may get lost a few times before you actually find it." It wasn't exactly an overwhelming endorsement. Fortunately, I soon learned that not only beauty, but apparently preferences in flea markets is in the eye of the beholder. I was thrilled with the Villeurbanne market, junk or not, of which there was plenty. But there were also treasures, which appeared to be waiting just for my arrival. This little white puffing and casing dress had "Martha Pullen" written all over it.

Upon close examination of this little puffing beauty, I discovered that absolutely every inch of it was stitched by hand. It is a basic mid-yoke style, but there is absolutely nothing basic about the yoke embellishment. French lace edging was applied in a curved manner around the neckline and the armscye. I've seen lace like this positioned around the neckline, but never around the armscye. Both pieces are attached to tiny baby Swiss entredeux on either side. The entredeux used throughout the dress construction is the tiniest I have ever seen. The batiste quality is quite high, it is sheer but with a dense stitch

count. The lace insertion used on the dress is 1 inch wide, and the puffing strips are 1-1/4 inch wide. The neckline is finished with baby entredeux with slightly gathered 1/2 inch wide French edging. Two rows of 1 inch wide puffing joined with entredeux run the width of the front yoke; tiny pieces of straight batiste fill in where the rounded French lace insertion begins to curve around the neckline. There is a casing of double batiste at the bottom of the puffing strips to run with ribbon. This casing is 1-3/8 inch wide and carries a ribbon around to the back of the dress, which ties in a bow. This same 1-3/8 inch wide batiste casing finishes the bottom of the puffed sleeves; a 2 inch wide casing serves as the skirt hem. How do I know that the hem was meant for more ribbon? There was an opening similar to the sleeve opening in the exact center back. I inserted the pink ribbons to highlight the casings and show you the versatility of this design.

The back of the dress is exactly like the front except that it fastened with four buttons and button loops. It is so exquisitely constructed that one can hardly detect the batiste-covered buttons.

The puffing on the skirt is exactly 1-1/4 inches wide. Like that on the bodice, it alternates with baby entredeux. Just for fun, I randomly measured the puffing on both the bodice and the skirts at different places. The perfection of this maker's handwork is astounding. At every point I measured, the puffing was precisely 1-1/4 inch wide. The puffing is so perfectly hand rolled and whipped that it actually stands straight everywhere. Even though I found a few other things at the Villurbanne Flea Market, it would have been worth the trip to Lyon just to bring home this dress.

Peach Smocked Boy's Romper
English, circa 1920

One of my favorite antique dealers in London is Stephen Lunn. He has stores all over the city including a Saturday stall at Portobello Road in one of the nicer indoor antique malls. On a typical trip to London, I will climb into one of those wonderful black cabs and frequent all of Stephen's stores in search of the perfect clothing or linens. I found this peach broadcloth suit at one of his stores. It is one of the most interesting of all of my boy's garments, since it has so many truly unusual sewing details.

The front suit fullness was gathered in at the shoulders with four rows of cable stitches smocked in blue and white. An embroidered running stitch was worked down the center garment along with two little squares that could be mistaken for buttons from a distance. A gathered 1/2 inch wide ruffle trims the batiste collar. The straight sleeves look to be three-quarter length and are finished in a 1 inch wide batiste cuff. Another 1/2 inch wide ruffle was inserted at the cuff-to-sleeve seam. The sleeves were inserted using flat felled seams. The inside seams are French.

Two patch pockets trimmed with blue running stitch were positioned below the waist on either side of the suit. More decorative blue running stitch was worked along the top of the leg cuffs at the bottom of the suit. The waist was cinched with a 1-1/2 inch wide belt, which is actually an extension of the back waistband. It fastens with a single pearl button in front.

What I find highly unusual about this suit are the openings, and I do mean "openings" plural. The pants not only button on and off at the waist, they were constructed with button openings down the sides of each leg. The crotch was sewn closed, but there is another slit left open in the lower front, which I assume was for bathroom purposes.

The back bodice of the suit closes with four pearl buttons and buttonholes. The total length of the suit is 20 inches.

Seven Sections Christening Dress

English, circa 1870

Seven sections might seem a peculiar name for such a beautiful antique dress; however, I looked and looked at the use of so many Swiss embroidered pieces in the center V and decided it was most appropriate. The limited adornment is its charm. Save for a series of tucks at the bottom, the skirt is completely unembellished. The eye focuses on the bodice – the area closest to the baby's face.

The dress was constructed of white batiste, the bodice of a series of white Swiss embroideries, including a beading, an all-over design and a border. It would have been made later than the mid-1850s because that is when Swiss embroideries of this type were first manufactured. The trims were applied to the bodice in a wide V that nearly stretches from shoulder seam to shoulder seam and dips down to create a bodice that is much longer than the bodices on most gowns in my collection. This section would have been created separately then placed on the bodice piece. The treatment traces somewhat of a boat neckline in front. Pretty Swiss trim flatters the neckline and was used again on both the top and bottom of the sleeve band. The sleeves are, short, straight and were attached without gathers. The dress closes in the back with casings at the neck and waist and a very narrow pull tape—more narrow than any of my other dresses.

The long and simple skirt was styled with five tucks above the hem. The center tuck is 1 inch wide; the sets of two tucks on either side of this larger tuck are 1/4 inch wide with 5/8 inch between them. The back placket opening is 12 inches; the overall length of the dress is 42 inches. The circumference of the skirt is 78 inches. The bodice of this dress and the side seams of the skirt were completely constructed by hand. The skirt tucks and the hem were stitched by machine.

Take this white vesture for a token of the innocence, which by God's grace in this holy sacrament of Baptism, is given unto thee.

—Prayer Book of Edward VI, 1549

Angled Swiss Insertion Dress
Australian, circa 1915

This piece has to be one of my favorite acquisitions. I found the white batiste and Swiss embroidery dress during an excursion to Melbourne, Australia. The antique store was a 45 minute cab ride from my hotel, and when I finally arrived I found it filled with glassware, furniture, maps, silver and other collectibles. I had just about decided my trip was in vain when I noticed a flight of stairs. The descent led me to the basement, and in the far end of the room, I spotted a display of white clothes. My "find" yielded this magnificent heirloom piece.

I'd never seen insertions placed in this manner— on top of tiers of tucks and positioned at vertical angles around the body of the skirt. As is typical of a turn-of-the-century child's dress, the sleeves are three-quarter length and trimmed with Swiss insertion and gathered Swiss edging. The two layered bottom ruffle was gently gathered as a single layer before applying to the bottom of the skirt as a finish. The same gathered Swiss edging repeats around the decorative high yoke. A coordinating, but narrower Swiss edging trims the neckline.

The Swiss edging around the neckline was trimmed to 1-1/4 inches wide and attached with a 1/4 inch wide bias binding, which serves as a casing. A cotton ribbon runs through the casing to make the neckline adjustable to the size of the child.

The yoke was tucked horizontally with two sets of three tucks. The tucks were folded 1/8 inch wide with 1/8 inch between individual tucks and 1 inch between the two sets. Five strips of 1 inch wide Swiss insertion were placed vertically across the yoke directly on top of the tucks. They were double topstitched, achieving a twin needle effect along the sides, and folded at the top to form a point. Gathered Swiss edging was applied entirely around the yoke. The Swiss-to-yoke join was concealed with a narrow, flat decorative bias trim.

The sleeves feature two sets of three tucks of the same width and with the same spacing as the bodice. The bottom of the sleeves were finished in a single piece of Swiss insertion and a slightly gathered Swiss edging, which matches the edging around the neckline.

The fabric for the skirt was tucked first with four sets of three tucks. As on the bodice, the individual tucks were folded to a 1/8 inch width and the sets were placed 1 inch apart. The angled Swiss insertion on the skirt matches the insertion on the bodice, however it is 1-3/4 inches wide, as opposed to 1 inch. These angled strips were folded to point at the very top and applied with double stitching.

The circumference of the dress, not counting the bottom ruffles is 58 inches and the length is 20-1/2 inches. The bottom double ruffle was tiered by widening the lower Swiss edging with a 2-1/2 inch piece of batiste. It is interesting to note that the Swiss trims do not match exactly, but coordinate beautifully—a tip for anyone working with heirloom trim. An exact match is not always preferable, and in fact a combination of trims can be truly exquisite.

The back of the dress is identical to the front, which is relatively unusual since limited materials and time often tempted the seamstress to cut corners. Buttons do not even disrupt the flow of the back; hooks and cloth eyes serve to close the hidden back placket. In all of my collection, very few pieces have hooks and eyes for closures.

Handkerchief Sleeve Trousseau Nightgown

American, circa 1920

The style and construction of this square-neck nightgown indicate that it was made somewhere between 1910 and 1930. A copy of *Illustrated Needlework* from 1923 features a number of nightgowns similar to this one.

I purchased the Handkerchief Sleeve Trousseau Nightgown in Massachusetts at an elegant show, which precedes the Brimfield Markets three times a year. There are several dealers at this show who specialize in beautiful vintage pieces. This particular nightgown was identified as a trousseau piece. The front V piece, below the high yoke lace bodice, and the shoulder trim were made partially from pieces of a handkerchief, which was embellished with French lace.

The slightly puffed sleeves were made from an entire handkerchief. The seamstress framed the handkerchief with rows of French beading and insertion. It appears as if she simply cut a circular opening in the center of the handkerchief and then attached it. Pale blue ribbons were run through both rows of beading to gather the sleeve around the arm. On the edge of the Swiss embroidered handkerchief was added a 1-inch wide insertion and two rows of 1-1/4 inch wide edging overlapped and straight

stitched together. The same three rows of French lace serve as both the neckline handkerchief trim and the pieces, which go over the shoulder. The laces were mitered at the corners.

The bodice of the gown is comprised of French edging, beading, insertion, beading, insertion, beading and insertion. There is another row of beading on top of the fabric portion where the skirt joins the lace-mitered bodice. Circular pieces of Swiss embroidery on organdy are at either side of this lace bodice; gathered French edging was gathered and stitched around the organdy circles. The circles are 1-1/2 inches in diameter. There is a very interesting detail on the right front organdy circle. It is embellished with a little silk ribbon flower with leaves, which was applied with hand stitching. Pale blue ribbon runs through all of the beading on the bodice, and it was hand stitched down to the gown.

The 1 inch wide hem, over which lies a 6-inch wide plain ruffle, was secured with a straight sewing machine stitch. The back of the gown features the mitered lace and organdy circles but does not have the handkerchief/lace piece that is found on the front. The total length of the gown is 55 inches.

*I*t isn't vanity that makes daughter (or mother, too)

want pretty trimmings and edgings on lingerie—it's just the

love of the beautiful with which all feminity is endowed.

—*Illustrated Needlework*, May 1923

ℒoops of Netting Blouse
Australian, circa 1900

My first teaching trip to Australia was in 1987 sponsored by my friend, Gloria McKinnon. Gloria loves vintage things as much as I do, and she always saves a day for us to go antiquing during my visit. On this first trip, Gloria drove me to a shop outside of Sydney that specializes in vintage clothing and linens, and it was there I purchased this Loops of Netting Blouse.

I can be assured the blouse is circa 1900 because it is a pigeon breasted silhouette with a secured waistline. What sets it apart from others of the era is that instead of attaching a collar to the neckline, it is simply outlined with a double row of netting trim. According to my research, most blouses and dresses of the pigeon breasted silhouette were made with medium to high collars.

The components of the blouse are a cotton netting over blouse and a full cotton lining. The layers float separately, but join at the neckline. There is a 1-1/4 inch wide piece of English lace insertion shaped and mitered in several places on the

high yoke of the blouse; this lacework travels around the blouse. Netting with sets of released tucks 3-1/2 inches long lends fullness to the bottom part of the blouse. The released tucks are 1/4 inch wide and were spaced 1/4 inch apart in four sections. The back of the blouse has two sets of three tucks.

The folded netting piece, which fashions loops on the blouse, was slightly gathered before shaping and stitching to the over-blouse. Three loops trim the bodice front; there is one on each sleeve and two in the back. A different netting loop technique trims the bottom of each sleeve with one loop on each cuff. The sleeves are very full at the bottom, which was also typical of this era. The back of both the blouse and the under-blouse close with hooks and eyes. The finished waist circumference when I fasten the hooks and eyes is 22 inches. The netting portion of the blouse was constructed totally by hand. The under blouse was made by machine.

$\mathscr{S}$wiss Embroidery Motif on Organdy
Iris & Leaves
Swiss, circa 1880

Embroidered Swiss motifs like this one are extremely rare. Fairly recently, I purchased a small collection of them, each one different. When I first examined this collection, I thought the antique motifs would be lovely to digitize for machine embroidery. The more I looked at them, however, the more complicated they seemed—quite possibly too intricate to stitch out on an embroidery sewing machine. After discussing the options with Angela Atherton, our machine embroidery artist and designer, she assured me it could be done. Pictured is one of the original pieces.

When looking at the original design, I named this one Iris, since it closely resembles an Iris. There is a good possibility that a particular flower was not intended, but rather a floral abstract when this piece was made. The embroidery is heavily padded satin stitch with French round thread lace inserted behind cutwork areas. The design was stitched on a piece of organdy, which is about 5 inches larger around than the actual design. That would give a seamstress ample room to insert the embroidery into her project leaving extra fabric for the rest of the garment or table linen design.

For a machine embroidery approach, you can use the "cutwork" option to cut away the organdy and insert pieces of French lace behind. It would be equally beautiful stitched and with nothing in the "open areas."

Lace machinery was introduced into Switzerland by the 1850s; however embroidery machines continued to be the mechanism of choice in that country. Machine Swiss embroidery was a well-established industry in the St. Gallen region of Switzerland by the 1850s and continues today. Martha Pullen Company has always imported embroideries and Swiss batiste from this particular region of Switzerland.

Puyallup Skirt
American, circa 1910

Every year I attend the Sewing Expo in Puyallup, Washington at the Washington State Fairgrounds. It is the largest sewing show in the country and is presented by Washington State University. The little town of Puyallup is very quaint and still remains somewhat frontier in its facade. I always go a day early to shop the antique stores on and off Main Street. There is one particular antique mall off the beaten path that I make a point never to miss. I specifically remember the day I found this skirt there, because I had just run into several ladies who recognized me from my *Martha's Sewing Room* television program.

One lesson I have learned, through years of searching every nook and cranny of antique stores and street markets, is that interesting items can turn up in any stall or booth. I never dismiss a store because a quick walk through reveals nothing of immediate interest. When I found what I call my Puyallup Skirt, I had searched the store almost completely uncovering few treasures, when I decided to take the two-flight walk up to the second floor. I really hadn't expected to find a thing, when something white caught my eye in the very back booth. I dug out what at first glance appeared to be a petticoat, and then realized I had actually unearthed a beautiful skirt made of a Swiss embroidered fabric. The skirt is 30 inches long and 72 inches in circumference. The waistline measures 25 inches.

I have a very specific reason for wanting to include this skirt in my book. If you look closely at the all-over embroidery, you will notice embroidered teardrop shapes framing lace fabric inserts. I have always referred to this technique as Australian Windowpane named after a blouse I purchased in Australia that was embellished with the same type of work. Basically, if you wanted to insert lace behind a pretty shape, you would simply outline the shape with a slight zigzag stitch, cut away the fabric, insert the lace behind the cut out, zigzag over the fabric again, and trim excess lace from behind.

Ecru Silk Middy Dress
American, circa 1920

Unraveling the era of middy dresses has been a relatively simply task for me since my antique magazines extensively feature the middy style for both women and children. In one magazine called *Illustrated Needlework* from 1923, most of the dresses featured for women and children were of the middy style.

This particular ecru silk middy was made for a child. I purchased it at the Nashville Flea Market. Finding an antique child's dress made of silk is always a rare treat for me because silk is one natural fiber that does not traditionally hold up very well over time. This piece does have some flaws, but overall is in very good condition.

A crudely embroidered flower bouquet stands alone at the center front of the dress. The fullness of the bodice was controlled with five sets of 1/8-inch wide released tucks spaced 1/8 inch apart across what would traditionally be the yoke area. The center set consists of five tucks; the two sets on either side are four tucks. Columns of French lace insertion each folded back to a point at the bottom were applied between the sets of tucks. A strip of French ecru insertion topped with a matching edging finishes the top of the neckline. The same tucks and lace

treatment is found on the back of the dress. The dress closes with five buttonholes and buttons.

The puffed sleeves were finished in a very pretty cuff, which is a combination of two 1/8 inch wide tucks, a piece of 3/4 inch wide ecru French lace insertion and a single tuck on the bottom fabric edge. The cuffs close with three buttons and three button loops.

Around the dropped or middy waistline, there is a gorgeous piece of 1 inch wide ecru Swiss beading, which was applied with entredeux on both sides. Ecru ribbon is run through the beading and ties in the back of the dress.

Centered on the skirt, is an embellishment of two 1/8 inch wide tucks, a strip of 1 inch wide ecru insertion and another set of two tucks. The 2 inch deep hem is secured with a straight machine stitch.

The quality of the machine sewing almost fooled me into believing the dress was partially hand stitched, because the stitching is very uneven. Upon closer look, I concluded that it was just sewn on a very poor machine, which formed slightly slanted stitches. The inside seams are regular seams, not French. The total back length of the dress is 28 inches. The circumference of the skirt is 90 inches.

Organdy Ruffle Dress
American, circa 1915

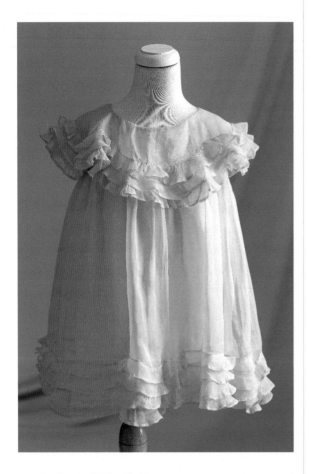

My Organdy Ruffle Dress is ever so precious and would be both easy and inexpensive to reproduce. It is pink, of course. The neckline on the high yoke is scooped just enough for a little girl's head to slip through, alleviating the need for any type of closure. The straight sleeves are practically hidden underneath the rows of ruffles on the organdy collar. The finished collar is 6 inches wide at center front. The three tiers of ruffles, which are sewn completely around, almost appear in motion due to the slight scallop along the collar edge. Each ruffle is 1 inch wide. The bottom ruffle was applied toward the bottom of the collar, with the second and third tiers stitched one on top of the next. The bottom edges were finished with a tiny double fold, which was machine straight-stitched. The top of the ruffles were simply folded under, gathered and straight stitched to the collar leaving a raw edge on the underside. The short sleeves were finished in a simple, 3/4 inch deep machine hem.

The bottom of the dress is slightly scalloped and trimmed with four tiers of ruffles. They were cut the same width and constructed exactly the same way as those around the collar of the dress. The length of the dress is 19-1/2 inches; the circumference of the skirt is 60 inches. The back of the dress is identical to the front.

If you belong to the lucky folk who can embroider the sheerest fabrics, and work with a fairy needle and finest cotton, you can make a baby's frock or cap look as if it were blown straight from fairyland.

—Fairy Craftmanship for Tiny Frocks
Baby Trousseau Book, circa 1920

Linen Boy's Dress
English, circa 1880

I wonder how many of you are aware that both boys and girls wore dresses until around 1900? There was a conscious effort to dress children in genderless clothing when they were very small. I picked up this simple white linen dress thinking it might have been a girl's pinafore of some sort. The more I study it, however; the more I believe it to be a little boy's summer dress. The linen is heavy. The sleeves are a kimono style, cut as one with the garment. Hand scalloped buttonhole stitch is the sole trim with the exception of a tiny, oblong flower and leaf wreath worked at the edge of each sleeve. A slit allows the buttonhole scallop to continue into sleeve for a bit of effortless detail,

framing the floral embroidery on two sides. The embroidery was entirely worked by hand.

A deep hem around the neckline shadows through the linen. It was secured with a machine stitch, and because of the embroidered scallop finish, it gives an effect similar to Maderia appliqué. It also serves as a neck facing. The side French seams were stitched by machine. The inverted V inserts on the skirt of the dress, though outlined in embroidered scallops, are a still a more tailored gesture. It is for this reason, I include this piece among my boy's garments.

The neckline opening is large enough to slip over the child's head with no need for a placket or buttons. The length of the dress is 22-1/2 inches.

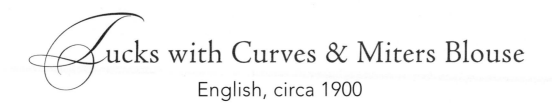

Tucks with Curves & Miters Blouse
English, circa 1900

Travel with me to the New Caledonian Market in Bermondsey very early Friday morning. True success in finding treasures at this market can never be guaranteed if one does not arrive by 5 am. Originally this market was the old Caledonian Market and was set up on Copenhagen Fields, Islington.

This particular Friday morning, I stumbled upon an elaborately embellished woman's blouse; it is a virtual study in lace shapes and tucking. I've seen lots of lace shaping on Victorian blouses, but this unconventional approach is indeed intricate and unique. To me, it was a work of passion by someone who purely loved to sew. Lace insertion that is both curved and mitered maps out a shape I've never seen before. The interior of the lace shaping is filled with tucks that extend and release beyond the lower outline of the lace shaping; they measure 1/8 inch wide and are spaced 1/8 inch apart. The short released tucks begin at the armscye of the blouse, and the long release tucks end about 4 inches from the waistband.

The front lace shaping was accomplished by working in three sections. The top piece is a square shape centered below the neckline and flanked by two V shapes. All the corners were mitered. The second lace shape is a series of curves or shallow scallops – a large centered curve, a slight, short curve and a medium length curve to the shoulders creates a faux yoke. The released tucks begin below the lace shaped "yoke." The third lace shaped section snakes from the center scallop of the "yoke" piece down to approximately 5 inches above the waistband, then loops back up the blouse where it is mitered and positioned in a 3-1/2 inch horizontal line at the center; the lace continues in a mirror image up to the other side of the yoke. Another unusual feature of this blouse is that Swiss entredeux was run right down the center of the tucked fabric dividing one side from the other. The tucks fold outward from the entredeux on either side.

The high collar consists of three rows of tucks, lace insertion and three more rows of tucks. Gathered French edging finishes the neckline at the very top, and Swiss entredeux joins the collar to the blouse.

The fitted 9-1/2-inch long cuffs are defined by six sets of 1/8 inch wide tucks with 1/8 inch in-between the tucks and insertion lace between the sets of tucks. They are finished with a slightly gathered white edging and joined to the sleeve with entredeux. Two buttonholes with loops close the cuff tightly around the wrist.

The back of the blouse was fashioned with two rows of lace shaping; the first has miters and the second curves. The back is closed with 16 small handmade buttonholes and pearl buttons. Swiss entredeux served to close the shoulder seam and to set in the puffed sleeves. The blouse is gathered to a fitted waistband.

Swiss Ayrshire Christening Dress
English, circa 1840

I have had the privilege many times of visiting my favorite museum in the world, the Bethnal Green Museum of Childhood in Bethnal Green, a suburb of London. The curator, Noreen Marshall has become a dear friend. Her wealth of knowledge in children's costume overwhelms me, and her willingness to share is just as generous. One of her favorite things to share is how creative Victorian women were and how thrifty they had to be, never letting anything go to waste until it was totally unusable. We love to make heirlooms today to be passed down from generation to generation. In Victorian times, the mothers who inherited the gowns from past generations would sometimes change them slightly to be more in keeping with the style of the day.

This beautiful white-on-white dress would be correctly identified as a "conversion dress." It was originally constructed around 1840, and later redesigned somewhat to suit the styles of 1890. What was converted? If you look closely around the neckline you can make out the original scooped neck Ayrshire dress with short sleeves typical of christening dresses from 1800-1880.

I completely fell in love with this gown when I purchased it in Cheltenham. Although there are some tears in the fabric, it is still in wonderful condition, and it was made completely by hand including the magnificent Ayrshire embroidery.

In the front V panel, a tiny V point extends past the waistline about 1 inch. Tradition has it that this V panel would have been left out for the christening of a male child and tucked in for a female. I have not verified this historically; however, I have had many people tell me this including some of my vendors in flea markets in both England and France. Construction details include a generous use of entredeux, which was used to join the V center bodice panel and the edgings on the outside. It also served to join the V panels on the top portion of the sleeve. The original short sleeves were fashioned from four pieces of Ayrshire embroidery—one V piece joined with hand entredeux stitched into the edge, and three more edgings of varying widths.

Some people speculate that the nuns in convents embroidered the Ayrshire garments of this era. After doing some research on Ayrshire hand embroidery,

Originally constructed around 1840, and later redesigned somewhat to suit the styles of 1890, this beautiful white-on-white dress would be correctly identified as a "conversion dress."

I found that a Mrs. Jameison, who lived in Ayr, Scotland, around 1814, was an entrepreneur who ran a cottage industry for Ayrshire in her hometown. The demand was so great that more was sold than could be produced. The designs to be embroidered were stamped onto the fabric and then sent out to the workers to complete at home.

The American Civil War of the 1860s diminished the supply of raw cotton to weave the fabrics onto which the embroidery was worked. Swiss machines about this time were producing handwork imitations of the Ayrshire work, which proved less expensive than the handwork, and truly one could hardly tell the difference. Consequently, the hand industry ceased to flourish in Ayrshire.

Ayrshire is characterized with flowers, leaves and stems. The gorgeous open fillings were either eyelets or flower-like drawn work. Sometimes these holes were filled with cotton netting, or embroidered netting.

The neckline and sleeves on this dress were probably altered around 1890 when necklines became higher on christening gowns. The seamstress added long sleeves and a plain fabric piece in the neckline with a casing and a drawstring. The original dress also closed with a drawstring. The gown has remained with three drawstring casings; one on the new section at the top of the neckline, one at the original neckline, and one at the waistline. The original drawstring casing was embellished with satin stitching.

The sweet sleeve was defined around the bottom with two rows of gathered French lace edging. A gathered French edging was also stitched at the top of the modified neckline treatment. Both of these French lace edgings are very narrow in what I commonly call "baby lace."

The gown laps right over left and closes with loops and flat buttons covered with the batiste fabric from the original gown. The original gown is 45 inches long. With the neckline modification, it is 48 inches long. The total underarm sleeve length is 5-2/3 inches. The circumference of the skirt is 76 inches. The beautiful Ayrshire panel is 6 inches wide at the top, 26 inches wide at the bottom, and 38 inches long.

Ayrshire is characterized with flowers, leaves and stems. The gorgeous open fillings were either eyelets or flower-like drawn work. Sometimes these holes were filled with cotton netting, or embroidered netting.

The Prayse of the Needle

And thus, without our needle we
may see

We should without our bibs and
biggins bee,

No shirts or smockes, our
nakedness to hide,

No garments gay to make us
magnified.

—John Taylor, Early Seventeenth Century

One of my favorite pastimes in London in the inevitable search for more historic garments is attending an auction at Christie's on Old Brompton Road. Each time we have taken groups to London, the tour has included an evening reception provided by the lovely staff at Christie's and a private preview of the next day's auction. When I travel alone, I always inspect the auction goods the day before, and when textiles are offered, I've even been known to make a special trip abroad. This particular smock was purchased December 3, 1996 from Christie's. It was not dated, and I have been unable to determine when it might have been made. Despite it's origin's being lost somewhere in history, it remains one of my favorite pieces.

The fabric is very coarse linen, and the smock has a number of details that would look lovely on a reproduction garment for a child to wear today. Not all smocks had pockets. This one has two rounded pockets, each carefully embellished: two flat rows of cable stitching were worked along the top edges and a single row was worked around the curves. At the center, an embroidered letter "A" was encircled by a concentric design worked in featherstitching. The initial would have most likely been the first letter of the child's first name for whom the smock was originally made.

Two rows of featherstitching were used to enhance the collar at the top and bottom of the 1-inch binding. This same decorative stitch was worked across the front and back yokes -- forming nine little "Vs" in the front and eight in back -- and around the Peter Pan collar, which separates in back, to accommodate

the back-button smock. The back of the smock was completed with five fabric covered buttons and five buttonholes. The buttonhole placket and a single side of the placket housing the buttons was outlined with featherstitching.

The majority of the handwork on this piece is smocking. The front and back pieces were smocked with a variety of stitches including stem and outline placed together at the top, which is called a wheat stitch. Eight rows of cable stitching were worked underneath the wheat stitch, followed by another row of wheat stitch; eight rows of the tiniest featherstitching, again followed by a row of wheat stitch; seven rows of cable stitching, followed by two rows of featherstitching (1/4 inch apart), and finally a bottom row of wheat stitching.

The sleeve fullness, like that of the garment, is contained with smocking. Six rows were worked at the shoulder including outline, cable, stem, and featherstitch; seven rows were worked in the same stitches on the cuff of the sleeve. The cuff measures 2 inches wide and is embellished with a tightly placed featherstitch at the top and the bottom.

Every inch of the smock was made by hand. The inside construction seams are either flat felled, French or unfinished straight seams. The body of the garment was joined where the selvage met alleviating the need for a finishing treatment there. The length of the smock is 25 inches; the circumference around the bottom is 89 inches. The width of the Peter Pan collar is 2-1/4 inches and the length of one of the sleeves is 10-1/2 inches and the other is 12-1/2 inches. The 1/2 inch hem was secured with a featherstitch.

Lace Bow Camisole
English, circa 1900

On my first and only trip to Gloucester, England, I found a little shop, which had lots of antique lingerie, of a plain variety, hanging on racks in front of the shop. I was on a fast, three-day teaching tour before our exhibition at the Knitting and Stitching show at Alexander's Palace in London. Although I had been traveling to England since Joe and I married, this was really the first time I had shopped outside of the London area. It is there that I found the Lace Bow Camisole.

This white batiste camisole was made entirely by machine and incorporates French lace and Swiss embroidered beading trim into the design. I feel compelled to stop here and explain that the proper name for camisole, which was written in the pattern books around 1900 was "corset cover." *The Delineator*, November, 1902, described several corset covers and matching petticoats: *"Feminine taste has wisely discarded orthodox modes and unattractive lines in lingerie, and, with an extravagant use of ribbon, lace and French or English nainsook, has succeeded in achieving charmingly pretty effects. There is, doubtless, no portion of a woman's wardrobe that receives so much consideration as does her underwear, for in this she evinces her individual skill and originality. Much attention is paid to the materials used, and there is a wide choice offered in cambric, mazalea, longcloth, dimity, muslin and imported nainsook. Valenciennes and Mechlin lace edgings and insertion and the old time favorite point de Paris will always remain in their favor because of their durable and effective qualities. Needlework, too, plays an important part in decoration, as is exemplified in some of the illustrations shown in this article."*

The article went on to describe *"a chic little corset cover"* and a *"corset cover of fine white dimity, closed at the back."*

On this "corset cover," French beading run with ribbon gathers in the fullness both around the neckline and at the waistline. Below the strip of beading, the neckline was fashioned with 1/2 inch French edging, 1-1/2 inch French beading, and 1/2 inch French insertion. Even though it appears that ribbons were not used on the center front, the maker of the piece constructed this section using Swiss embroidered beading. Three rows of 1/2-inch insertion were applied from the bow lace motif on the front at an angle to the shoulder treatment.

The motifs on the front were pre-manufactured French motif lace bows, which were most likely designed for use on lingerie. The bows were straight stitched then hand whipped around the edges. To create a sleeve, the camisole was split on the shoulders before inserting a "tube" of four rows of 1/2 wide insertion with gathered 5/8 inch wide edging. The back of the camisole features a row of French edging at the top, the beading row with the ribbon run through it and three rows of French insertion. Another of the French bow motifs was straight stitched on top of these rows of lace and hand whipped around the edges.

The bottom was finished with a row of French beading and narrow edging. The covered placket in the front of the camisole conceals a closure of three buttons and buttonholes.

Pre-Purchased Panels Swiss Dress
American, circa 1910

In the late 1800s and well into the 20th century, Swiss companies manufactured panels, which were in essence pre-fabricated dresses. I believe this little white Swiss batiste dress was just that. All one needed to do was stitch the pieces together. Notice that the bodice and sleeves are all in one piece. The embroidery would have already been worked on the pre-purchased panel, a design may have been stamped on the panels, or a template may have been provided.

An embroidered edge that I like to call "scalloped scallops" lends distinction to the skirt hem. Sculpted around the delicate shaped edge is gathered French round thread lace. Less elaborate embroidered scallops finish the edges of the yoke, neckline and sleeves.

Three 3/8 inch wide tucks are folded into the body of the skirt, and eyelet embroidery drips down the center front of the gown into an expanded design above the center scallop. Two tiny eyelet flowers were worked just above the scallops to either side of the center scallop. The fullness of the sleeves is controlled in quite an unusual manner. Little pleats, six in all, were folded in and secured by three rows of straight stitching. This treatment shaped the sleeve to fit properly.

The back of the dress is all in one piece. A 6-1/2 inch long placket forms the opening, and the back is closed with one snap at the top. The length of the dress is 24 inches. The circumference is 56 inches at the bottom.

In an old Godey of seventy years ago I gazed, fascinated, at the illustration of infant clothes "in elegant simplicity." The skirt was fully a yard long and a mass of the most exquisite embroidery with short, puffed sleeves caught with slender chains of coral; it was a mother's adoring love that loaded the tender body with so heavy a burden! In this respect we are wiser than the mothers of yesterday. Take up the dress of today, delicate, and weightless... light and loose are the things of today, leaving the small limbs as ecstatically free and unhampered as a gamboling lamb's.

—*The Modern Priscilla*, July, 1922

Normandy Lace Heart Pillow
French, circa 1920

Being the romantic that I am, I love hearts, lace shaped or otherwise. Valentine's Day was always one of my favorite holidays and still is. Imagine how taken I was when I happened upon this Normandy lace heart pillow at the Paris Flea Market. It was discolored and in far from perfect condition, but I simply couldn't pass it up.

Normandy is a town in France where Normandy lace tablecloths were first made. The best description I can give you of this type of lacework is that it is similar to crazy patch. Different types of lace are basically sewn together creating a uniform design.

Netting, especially tulle, is used as a background for all types of embroidery. English laces are made on cotton tulle. Using the Normandy lace technique, beautiful wedding veils, curtains and bedspreads were made by embroidering on tulle. Netting is still made today, and with modern embroidery machines and water-soluble stabilizers, it is both rewarding and easy to recreate netting lace.

One can always depend on the French to make beautiful things and this pillow is no exception.

The focal point of my lace pillow is the netting piece encircled with 1 inch wide lace edging. It measures 6 inches in diameter. French lace is woven with gathering threads on one side, if it is edging, and on both sides if it is insertion. Laces can be shaped by pulling one of the guide or gathering threads. In this example, the edging circle would have been shaped and then applied on top of the embroidered netting motif.

The remainder of the pillow front is an all-over piece of netting lace, two strips of lace insertion radiating from the circle into the upper curves of the heart, and lace insertion outlining the pillow completely around the heart shape. The back of the pillow is the all-over netting lace. Lace edging measuring 1-1/2 inches wide was gathered around the outside of the pillow for an appropriate finishing touch. As lovely as the embroidered netting and Normandy technique is on this heart pillow, it can be equally appealing on heirloom sewn garments and other home decorative items.

Triple Triangle Christening Dress
English, circa 1880-1910

I purchased the Triple Triangle Christening Dress on my very first antique shopping trip to London's Portabella Road. This famous street has an estimated 2000 antique stall holders and shop owners, which produces an endless diversity and some true walking memories. It was there that I found this piece that I believe was originally worn as a christening dress.

The fabric is white Swiss batiste and the trims are white French lace edging and insertion. The wide French lace insertion is a round thread rose pattern and the round thread lace edging is a dot pattern. The number three appeared to have guided the design approach as there are several elements grouped to that effect. I suspect, as do many students of costume history that when a seamstress grouped embellishment in this manner it was an intentional representation of the Father, the Son and the Holy Spirit.

This particular piece was made by hand except for the double machine stitching of the bias tubing and the tucks. Three long, narrow fabric triangles were applied to the shoulder serving a decorative function. The triangles were fashioned out of a single piece of fabric and in all measure 3-1/2 inches across the shoulder. Each triangular section measures 1 inch at the base. French cotton edging 3/8 inch wide was straight stitched around each triangle section; the seamstress gathered the lace slightly as she approached the point of each triangle. She gathered the same French lace around the neckline of the dress.

The lowered neckline could be adjusted to fit with a drawstring pulled through a 1/4-inch bias casing.

The drawstring is a special type of very narrow cotton ribbon. Tiny French knots 1/16 inch apart were worked in a double row around this neckline casing and again around the bias binding at the waist. The waistline of the dress also houses a gathering ribbon.

The long sleeves were finished with two rows of gathered French edging with a row of French beading in between. It's quite reasonable to assume

that tiny ribbons were run through the beading in the sleeves of the dress and tied into a bow.

The front bodice V panel was embellished with a heavy 3/4 inch wide French round thread lace insertion, which was stitched together very carefully matching the large rose pattern. The total lace panel piece, if you were recreating this dress, would need to be 8-1/2 inches x 11 inches in order to cut out the shape for the bodice. (Once cut, it would require an an-

gular placement.) Rows of 1/8 inch wide bias tubing were applied in a crisscross pattern between each rose on the lace panel and secured with two rows of straight stitching on either side of the tubing. Pretty fabric pieces edged in 3/8 inch wide French lace flank the center panel almost like a middy collar. The edging was secured with a double row of tiny narrow French knots stitched at the fabric-to-lace join.

The skirt's fancy band is a series of three 1/8 inch tucks, a strip of the round bobbin rose insertion, further embellished with angular strips of 1/8-inch bias tubing stitched on between each rose, and another series of three tucks. The insertion was again securedwith double rows of French knots. The total length from the top tuck to the bottom of the skirt is 5 inches. The hem is 2 inches deep. Another

interesting detail of this dress is that the inside skirt seams are not French seams. They were simply stitched, by hand, and the selvages of the fabric were left exposed. This is unusual in a dress with this much hand detail. The back of the dress is plain with two buttons and tiny buttonholes. A very interesting fact about the back of this dress is that the opening, including the placket in the skirt, is 13 inches making it very easy to get the baby in and out of the dress. The dress is 42 inches long and the skirt measures 84 inches in circumference.

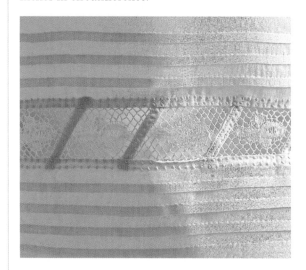

Many people thought that using groups of three sewing details indicated the *Father, Son, and Holy Spirit.*

Dutch Silhouette Romper
American, circa 1920

It's not difficult to see the Dutch influence in this pink embroidered boy's suit. In fact, the style was called the Dutch Silhouette Romper and was very prominent in the 1920s and 30s.

Indulge me while I abbreviate a story about how I acquired this and some of the cutest boy's things in my collection.

For several days, my husband Joe and I trudged through the muddy fields at the Brimfield Markets in Massachusetts. He had had just about enough, while I, as usual, was sure that just under the next tent I'd come upon the find of the century. With Joe tapping his watch and reminding me of our plane reservations for the flight home, I agreed to head toward the parking lot, when lo and behold I spotted several little "rag tag" boy suits hanging on the wall of a vendor's tent. Knowing how hard it was to find boy's heirlooms, Joe acquiesced to one more stop. The vendor not only showed me the things on display, she offered to sell me a garbage bag full of "musty old boy's things" sight unseen. Joe's skepticism over what I had purchased waned when I dug out this adorable suit on the plane ride home.

This suit looks to be about a size three. In a pattern book I have from 1919, it states that the Dutch silhouette rompers were "for children 1-5 years." This particular example is pink linen, with decorative blue stitching around the Peter Pan collar, but with age it has faded to a pale ecru. The front embroidery is a blue lazy daisy flower with a satin stitched yellow center dangling from black running stitch stems with lazy daisy leaves. Although the style appears to be a button off suit in front, it is not. The scalloped front waistband topped with two beautiful pearl buttons is simply a decorative feature. The sleeves are a kimono style, cut all on one with the top and are finished with a 1-1/2 inch wide cuff.

The Dutch-style triangular pockets were stitched into the suit with the top hemmed edge left open for inserting a little boy's hand. The same decorative stitching around the collar secures the pocket hem with a touch of blue thread.

The cuffs on the legs are 1-3/8 inch wide. The center back of this suit closes with three buttonholes and three buttons. The wide waistband does button off in back with five buttons and buttonholes. The crotch is stitched closed. The suit was machine made and the inside seams are French. The leg openings, which would have come almost to the knees on this style suit measure 11 inches in circumference. The sleeve cuff is 7 inches around. The total length of the suit is approximately 20 inches.

Sweet and Simple Daygown
American, circa 1920

Antiquing in my immediate area has produced some rewards, especially when I am diligent in my visits to the local antique stores. Now closed, the Five Points Antique Store consistently held treasures for my collection. I purchased this sweet white batiste daygown there many years ago. It would be simple to reproduce using the daygown pattern in my *Grandmother's Hope Chest* book.

The embellishment is at a minimum, letting baby be the focal point. Four 3-1/2 inches long released tucks were folded into each shoulder; they are 1/8 inch wide and 1/8 inch apart. Just below the center of the neckline, the dress is graced with a lace panel created with five pieces of white French lace folded back at the bottom to form a point. The lace alternates between 1 inch widths and 1/2 inch widths.

The lace panel was straight stitched to the daygown, and at center point, measures 3-1/2 inches long from the neckline.

The puffed sleeves and the neckline finish are a 1/4 inch wide bias binding and lightly gathered French lace. The back of the dress has two tucks on each side of the placket closing, which is 6-1/2 inches long. There is a single button and buttonhole at the neckline. The 4-1/2 inch wide hem was secured with a lovely hand hemstitching. Today's modern sewing machines and a wing needle entredeux stitch achieve the same effect in a fraction of the time. The dress was completely constructed by hand. All the seams are French, including the shoulder and sleeve inset. As sweet as this design is as a daygown, I envision it lengthened for a simple, yet elegant christening gown.

Since this little dress uses beautiful bias bands around the neckline and sleeves, I wanted to share a little historical snippet about bias bands that I found in the following paragraph in *Illustrated Needlework*, May, 1923:

To cut bias bands, fold the corner of the goods up so that the two straight edges of the triangle are the same length. Make a crease. Measure off the width the bands are to be and draw lines with a yardstick and tailor's chalk. Mark off as many bands as needed before cutting. Cut on the marks carefully, as the least change will throw the bands off the true bias. Bias bands of thin materials, like silk, should be made over crinoline before being used.

Martha's Earthquake Dress
American, circa 1900

In case you're wondering about the name of this garment, I purchased it in Puyallup, Washington not long before I experienced my first earthquake. It happened during an antique outing I was enjoying while my staff set up for an Expo at the Washington State Fairgrounds. I had already purchased this particular dress along with a few other things when all of a sudden the floor began to tremble, everything began to fall off the shelves, and I ran for the door. After I peered outside and saw the sidewalks roll-

ing and the cars following suit, I didn't know whether to go back into the store or head outside, so I played it safe and stood in the doorway clutching my bag of goodies. Needless to say, I survived along with this magnificent summer gown of sheer white batiste, hand embroidery, chemical lace and tucks.

This dress is feminine, classic and flattering to a woman's figure. Like most of the styles today, it is actually very formfitting in an elegant way. Pintucks were used to tame the fullness around the shoulders. They number 10 in front, seven in back; they were folded 1/16 inch wide and spaced 1/8 inch apart. The front V was made of two pieces of chemical lace insertion 2 inches wide with batiste and narrow 3/4 inch wide chemical insertions in the middle. The chemical lace most likely came from Switzerland and has an entredeux edge on each side with little picots at 1/2-inch intervals. The rounded neckline was encircled with two rows of chemical lace insertions. Another row of the insertion was used to form the 2 inch wide collar, which was held up by stays. The back of the dress was trimmed almost identically to the front and closed with hooks and eyes on the collar and round lace yoke, and with 11 buttons and buttonholes down the remainder of the back.

The waistband for this garment was simply fashioned by reinforcing a length of chemical lace with a batiste lining. A series of 1/8 inch wide released tucks placed 3/8 inch apart served to gather the fullness of the skirt to the waistband; the tucks were placed in sets of seven. Two sets of four tucks were worked into the design of the fitted sleeves; they are 1/16 inch wide tucks placed 1/8 inch apart with 1 inch between the sets. A floral, hand embroidered motif was worked on the sleeve's between the tucked section and the sleeve band, which was made out of another piece of the chemical lace insertion.

The bulk of the hand embroidery on this dress was worked in an extensive padded satin stitch combined with additional classic embroidery stitches. The hand work was made even more interesting through the use of lace inserts worked into the designs. I believe the inserts were purchased chemical lace motifs.

The best way to determine whether lace or embroidery is machine or hand wrought is to examine the backside. When I turned this piece over, I found a clue in the asymmetry of the work—on the "matching designs" some had different sized leaves, others did not have

threads crossing over at the same places, and none of them had identical stitch placement. If you are ever in doubt concerning the embroidery being hand or machine made, turn the garment over. A magnifying glass may be necessary to see intricate details, but in the case of my earthquake dress, I only needed to find matching pieces of the embroidery to realize that the work wasn't uniform enough to be machine made. It was only after I had a chance to examine the garment did I realize what a treasure this piece truly was. The fabric is very delicate. The basic construction was done on a machine, including the straight stitched 2 3/4-inch hem and the inside French seams. It has always seemed peculiar to me that on nearly all of my Victorian-era dresses, even those that were primarily handmade, the hems were straight stitched by machine. It appears to have been the customary treatment of the time.

> *If you are ever in doubt concerning the embroidery being hand or machine made, turn the garment over…In the case of my earthquake dress, I only needed to find matching pieces of embroidery to realize that the work wasn't uniform enough to be machine made.*

The tiniest of waistlines on a Victorian era dress is an indication that it was worn with a corset. Corsets were often pulled so tightly during this time that it wasn't unusual for a woman to faint from an inability to breathe properly.

$\mathscr{S}$imple Handstitched Baby Dress
English, circa 1915

If you were to ask me, "Martha, what is the most beautiful place you have ever visited?" several places would come to mind. If you insisted I choose one, however, I would have to say Bath, England. I never tire of my fascination with this historic town. The magnificent Abbey was started in 1499. Bath's revival was caused by three men—Richard Nash, a gambler, Ralph Allen, an entrepreneur and John Wood, an architect. They planned and oversaw in the 1700s the building and renovation of this glorious city.

Pulteney Bridge, where I purchased my Simple Hand Stitched Baby Dress, was designed by Robert Adam in 1771 following a competition among architects. It is the only bridge in England with shops on both sides. Those shops are still in existence today, and I always find treasures in them.

This precious white batiste dress was stitched totally by hand with meticulous stitching. Many people mistakenly believe that all of the Victorian white baby dresses were for christenings. They were not. Babies wore this type of dress until they were old enough to walk. Certainly any of the dresses could have been used for a christening; however, most of the less ornate dresses were worn as everyday baby clothes.

This little dress is 32 inches long and has a circumference of 60 inches. The high yoke neckline is finished with a bias band a scant 1/4 inch wide. The band is topped with featherstitching, which was stitched by hand. That alone would be a beautiful finish around the neck of a baby dress, then, or now. This one, however is further embellished with a 1/2 inch wide White French Cluny lace, slightly gathered and whipped to the top of the binding.

The sleeves are 8 inches long and were rolled and whipped at the bottom to a pretty little piece of Swiss insertion. The same French Cluny lace as trims the neckline is slightly gathered and whipped to the bottom side of this Swiss insertion.

The front and back yokes alternate rows of 5/8 inch wide white batiste with featherstitching down the center and white French Cluny lace insertion, also 5/8 inch wide. The gathered skirt joins the bodice in an interesting way. A bias binding topped with featherstitching was first sewn to the bottom of the fancy yokes, then the skirt was merely folded over, gathered, and whipped to the bias binding. This 1/2-inch "folded over" portion was left unfinished on the interior of the dress. I have seen this technique used before, leaving a much wider piece of fabric. I can only assume it was used for lengthening the dress at a later time.

The back of the dress closes with two buttons and two buttonholes. The alternation of batiste and lace strips across the back strips was planned so that the two batiste strips meet at center back, serving as the perfect foundation for stitching buttons and buttonholes. The outside batiste strip on the back where the handmade buttonholes are found is also trimmed with hand featherstitching. The total back placket opening is 6 inches long.

The bottom of the skirt is sweet and simple. Two sets of two hand-stitched tucks were worked across the skirt near the bottom. The tucks are 1/8 inch wide, with 1/8 inch spacing between them.

Swiss insertion joins a hand rolled and whipped ruffle to the bottom of the dress. French Cluny lace, stitched flat to the bottom of the ruffle, provides the finishing touch. The ruffle is 2-1/2 inches wide.

Australian Embroidered Child's Dress
Australian, circa 1910

My incredible travel opportunities to teach sewing have taken me to six continents. On most of those journeys, I have factored in time to browse antique stores in hopes of finding the perfect piece to add to my collection. On my first trip to Melbourne, Australia, I hit the jackpot. I found not one, but several Australian heirloom dresses of museum quality. This child's dress was among the items I purchased that trip, and it has to be one of my favorites solely for the embroidery.

This white-on-white embroidered dress is so elegant and yet so simple. Every stitch was sewn by hand, construction and embroidery. Embroidery adorns the skirt and high yoke in front and back. The delicate, long sleeves were finished with a wrist band of Swiss entredeux, a strip of fabric with two 1/16 inch wide tucks, more Swiss entredeux and gathered white French lace edging, which is 3/8 inch wide. Swiss entredeux was used at the shoulder seams, and again to join the sleeves to the bodice and the skirt to the bodice. It was also used around the neckline of the dress before gathered French edging was applied. Entredeux means "between the two" and it was certainly used to its fullest capacity in this little masterpiece.

Large, 1-inch buttonholes placed 1-1/4 inches apart were worked at the base of the front and back yokes through which a ribbon sash was run. The original sash was not with the dress when it was purchased, so I added the 1-inch silk satin ribbon. White work flowers and satin stitched round dots were worked in-between the buttonholes. Beautiful sprays of padded satin stitch flowers and little leaves were scattered on both the front and back bodices.

The embroidery on the skirt is beyond magnificent. On the original embroidery there is drawn work inside the flower wreaths connected to the larger bows. You might substitute white cotton netting for the same gossamer feeling, or you could stitch out wing needle entredeux pieces to use as inserts.

If you are hand stitching the embroidery, you could certainly shadow embroider the bows. The remainder is satin stitching except for the bottom scallops, which call for a buttonhole stitch. Any basic, slightly dropped yoke pattern could be used to make a reproduction dress. The back closes with three buttons and buttonholes, which are hidden by an outside casing. The total

back opening of the dress is 9 inches including the placket in the skirt. The total length of the dress is 19 inches. The circumference of the skirt is 62 inches.

Victorian Nightdress with Ruffles
American, circa 1900

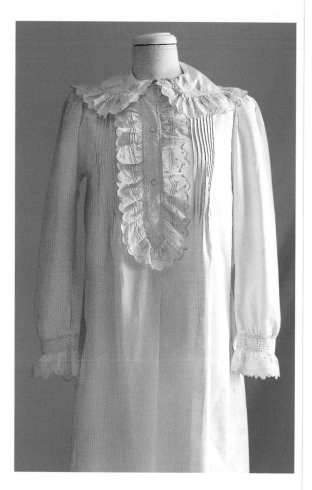

This Victorian nightdress is very typical of women's sleepwear of the Victorian and Edwardian era. It is white linen and is beautifully detailed. The portrait collar and front placket are outlined with a gathered 2 inch wide Swiss embroidered edging. The skilled seamstress knew that as she approached the corners or points, she needed to factor in more gathers so that the collar would lay properly. She also incorporated three 1/16 inch wide tucks placed 1/16 inch apart into the edging to further control the shaping. The front placket is 16 inches long and 6 inches wide and on each side are eight folded, released tucks measuring 1/8 inch wide and placed 1/8 inch apart. The puffed sleeves are finished at the cuff with four folded 1/8 inch wide tucks between two rows of Swiss insertion; gathered and tucked Swiss edging trims the bottom. The side seams are flat felled, which is typical of nearly all of the nightdresses in my collection. This type of seam was strong and durable for a garment that was worn and washed frequently. The circumference of the bottom of the skirt is 74 inches. The length of the gown is 54 inches.

Embroideries

The embroidery designs shown are a sampling of the many patterns featured on the antique garments. These may be enlarged for hand embroidery or are available for machine embroidery (all formats) on CD-ROM from Martha Pullen Company.

Australian Embroidered
Child's Dress

Australian Embroidered
Child's Dress

Australian Embroidered
Child's Dress

Australian Embroidered
Child's Dress

Australian Embroidered
Child's Dress

Australian Embroidered
Child's Dress

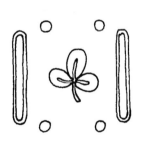

Australian Embroidered
Child's Dress

Australian Embroidered
Child's Dress

Australian Embroidered
Child's Dress

Australian Embroidered
Child's Dress

Australian Embroidered
Child's Dress

White Work Leaves &
Bows Baby Dress

English Middy Overlay
Dress

English Middy Overlay
Dress

English Middy Overlay
Dress

Victorian Pintucks
Dress

Long Netting Lace
Christening Cape

Long Netting Lace
Christening Cape

Long Netting Lace
Christening Cape

Long Netting Lace
Christening Cape

Oval Yoke Embroidery &
Tucks Baby Dress

Oval Yoke Embroidery &
Tucks Baby Dress

Swiss Embroidery Motif
on Organdy
Chrysanthemum & Leaves

Swiss Embroidery Motif
on Organdy
Iris & Leaves

English Embroidered Motif
Woman's Dress

English Embroidered Motif
Woman's Dress

English Embroidered Motif
Woman's Dress

Netting Dress
with Grapes

Lace Poetry Blouse

Lace Poetry Blouse

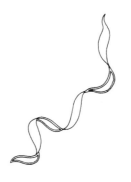

Lily of the Valley
White Coat

Lily of the Valley
White Coat

Lily of the Valley White Coat

Pre-Purchased Panels
Swiss Dress

Pre-Purchased Panels
Swiss Dress

Pre-Purchased Panels
Swiss Dress

French Boudoir Pillow

French Boudoir Pillow

French Boudoir Pillow

French Boudoir Pillow

French Boudoir Pillow

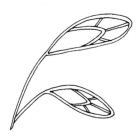

French Boudoir Pillow

French Boudoir Pillow

Normandy Lace Heart
Pillow

Bows & Flowers
Woman's Camisole

Bows & Flowers
Woman's Camisole

French Silk Christening
Ensemble

French Silk Christening
Ensemble

French Silk Christening
Ensemble

French Silk Christening
Ensemble

French Silk Christening
Ensemble